D0216966

Code Red in the Boardroom

Code Red
in the Boardroom

Crisis Management as
Organizational DNA

W. Timothy Coombs

Westport, Connecticut
London

Library of Congress Cataloging-in-Publication Data

Coombs, W. Timothy.
  Code red in the boardroom : crisis management as organizational DNA /
W. Timothy Coombs.
     p. cm.
  Includes bibliographical references and index.
  ISBN 0-275-98912-7 (alk. paper)
  1. Crisis management.   2. Communication in management.   I. Title.
  HD49.C663   2006
  658.4'056—dc22   2005034113

British Library Cataloguing in Publication Data is available.

Library of Congress Catalog Card Number: 2005034113
ISBN: 0-275-98912-7

First published in 2006

Praeger Publishers, 88 Post Road West, Westport, CT 06881
An imprint of Greenwood Publishing Group, Inc.
www.praeger.com

Printed in the United States of America

The paper used in this book complies with the
Permanent Paper Standard issued by the National
Information Standards Organization (Z39.48-1984).

10 9 8 7 6 5 4 3 2 1

To Sherry, for all her support with this project,
and to Mac, for being himself.

Contents

Preface

Read or watch the news and you know that organizations face crises every day. Some are small, and some are mammoth, but all can harm the unprepared organization. Crisis management is more than just a document. Throughout this book, I argue that true crisis management involves making it a part of the organization's DNA. Crisis management is what an organization *does*, not something it has. Great crisis managers know that the best way to manage a crisis is to avoid one. However, not all crises can be prevented, so managers must be prepared to deal with the reality that crisis is a matter of when, not if. The purpose of this book is to reinforce the need for crisis management and push organizations to make it a part of their DNA. Part I examines the main types of crises to illustrate the daily threats an organization may face. Part II provides advice on managing crisis and integrating crisis management into the organization's DNA. The appendixes provide additional practical tools and resources.

1

Introduction: Crises Do Happen, So Be Prepared

Since the terrorist attacks of September 11, 2001, American companies have been more aware that the world is a dangerous place. Even the best company is just a few steps away from a crisis. Companies should be prepared through crisis management. Unfortunately, the preparation is often more talk than action. Management takes a few surface actions and believes their company is ready to face a crisis. Or worse, only a few actions are taken because management thinks a crisis will not happen to them. To be effective, management must take crisis management seriously. Crisis management is not an extra to be *added on*. It needs to be something that an organization *is*. I refer to this as crisis management becoming part of a company's DNA. This chapter reviews the need for crisis management and the difference between crisis management as an add-on verses crisis management as DNA.

CRISES: DEFINITION AND DANGERS

We often use the term *crisis* lightly. It is a crisis when we misplace our keys, or the toner in the copier runs low. In corporate life, the word *crisis* should be reserved for specific events. A crisis is an unpredictable, major threat that can have a negative effect on the organization, industry, or stakeholders if handled improperly. Although we can anticipate that crises will occur, we do not know when they will happen. Crises are like an earthquake. We know one can hit but cannot predict exactly when. Crises threaten to disrupt a company's operation or demand significant resources—it is a major threat. Crises can result in negative outcomes, such as injuries, loss of life, loss of financial resources, property damage, environmental damage, and reputational damage.[1]

Humans are good at ignoring threats. We choose to ignore that certain actions, such as eating fatty foods, can cause health problems. Why do people still smoke or drink and drive when the dangers are well known? Management is only human and can choose to ignore that the company has crisis risks. In reality, companies are vulnerable to a wide array of crises. We can categorize crises into three groups: (1) attacks on an organization, (2) accidental actions that place stakeholders at risk, and (3) purposeful wrongdoing by management. A few examples will illustrate the vulnerability of companies to these types of crises.

In late 1999, Burger King ran a tie-in promotion with the popular cartoon and trading card game Pokémon. This was a marketing coup for Burger King, as the giveaway was a magnet attracting millions of children to the restaurants. In December, the joy turned to sorrow. On December 11, 1999, a thirteen-month-old girl in Sonora, CA, was found suffocated in her playpen by half of a Poke Ball (part of the giveaway). On December 27, Burger King announced the recall of the Poke Balls. The recall effort included full-page advertisements in *USA Today*. In January 2000, a four-month-old boy in Indianapolis suffocated in his crib because of a Poke Ball. Burger King intensified the recall with fifteen-second television advertisements. The recall effort was well beyond the government-required distribution of news releases. Experts speculated on its effects on Burger King's reputation and sales. Burger King maintained it had always informed consumers that the giveaways were for kids over the age of three.[2] However, this was little comfort in light of two deaths. Success of the tie-in quickly changed to a serious threat.

For most of 2004, a computer hacker had gained entry into wireless giant T-Mobile's servers. He accessed passwords, Social Security numbers, e-mail messages, and personal photos. Nicholas Jacobsen began selling people's identities, reading e-mails of U.S.

Secret Service agents using T-Mobile, and posting online personal photos taken by Hollywood celebrities Demi Moore, Paris Hilton, and Ashton Kutcher. The hack was known as early as March 2004. The government began active involvement with the case in July 2004 and began making arrests in October 2004.[3] T-Mobile was embarrassed by one hacker who had free rein through their sensitive data for over six months. T-Mobile, like most companies that were hacked, was reluctant to go to authorities for fear of public embarrassment and loss of customers.

Kinston, North Carolina, is the home to one of West Pharmaceutical's production facilities. That operation converts rubber into syringe plungers and intravenous fitments. The Kinston facility is brand new; it reopened in 2004. On January 29, 2003, an explosion leveled the old facility. There was no production for over a year. The greatest tragedy was not the destruction of the facility; it was the deaths of six employees. There is a permanent memorial to commemorate those workers. The cause of the accident was dust. Rubber dust had accumulated in a drop ceiling. Something ignited the dust, and the explosion leveled the facility. Any organic dust can lead to a massive explosion. West Pharmaceutical management had followed all the government guidelines for dust. In reality there are few dust regulations except for those governing the operations at grain silos. The rubber dust was a hidden danger just waiting to strike.[4]

No case may be stranger than the 2005 report of a fingertip in Wendy's chili. On March 22, 2005, Anna Ayala said she was eating chili at a Wendy's in San José, California. She felt something odd in her mouth and spit out a 1.5-inch fingertip. An investigation worthy of a *CSI* episode ensued. The fingertip was fingerprinted and DNA tested. All the workers from the restaurant were examined, and none were missing fingers. Similarly, no suppliers had employees report accidents with a lost finger. The finger was also evaluated to determine if it had been cooked or not. The finger was not cooked, indicating it was not part of the supply chain of ingredients for the chili. Wendy's first offered $50,000 then doubled the reward to $100,000 for information about the origin of the fingertip. Wendy's restaurants in northern California saw a major drop in business. Some employees were laid off, and some locations lost hundreds of thousands of dollars in business.

You probably know the rest of the story. Ayala herself had placed the fingertip in the chili. The fingertip was lost in a work-related accident by a friend of her husband. Wendy's management was thrilled when an arrest was made.[5] But the financial and reputational damage had been done. You've probably heard one or more Wendy's fingertip jokes. The lost revenues were no joke. A piece of finger coupled with greed created a major crisis for Wendy's.

Crises happen more frequently than we might think. Every day there are product recalls and industrial accidents. Product tampering and management misconduct are not uncommon. The point is that companies are vulnerable to a wide array of threats or potential crises. Management cannot afford to say, "That could never happen here." If you sell food, some day it might be contaminated through tampering or by accident. If you have a production facility, it could be the site of a horrific industrial accident. Any company can have management that misbehaves. Companies must be prepared for crisis. We call that preparation crisis management.

CRISIS MANAGEMENT: THE REAL PREPARATION

There are two basic objectives to crisis management: (1) prevent a crisis from occurring and (2) lessen the damage from a crisis if one does happen. Experts argue that all crises have warning signs.[6] A few minor accidents indicate that a major one could occur. Improper quality control checks could result in harmful products going to market. There were a series of small accidents at the Union Carbide facility in Bhopal prior to the worst industrial accident the world ever witnessed in 1984. Crisis managers work to find the warning signs and prevent the crisis. The problem is recognizing the warning signs. Sometimes it is hard to tell a signal is a warning sign until it is too late and the crisis erupts. As the saying goes, "Hindsight is 20/20." It is much easier to see the warning signs after a crisis than before. After a crisis, you know where an event is leading, but that may not be clear before the crisis. Before the crisis you have to project where an event might go. In emergency management, efforts to prevent crises are referred to as *mitigation*. Mitigation identifies and reduces risks.

Regardless of your best efforts to prevent crises, a few will sneak by. That is why crisis management also seeks to reduce the damage from the crisis. Crisis managers try to prevent injuries, deaths, financial loss, property damage, environmental damage, and reputational damage. Crisis managers seek to protect stakeholders, the organization, and the industry. Effective crisis management can reduce the physical and financial harms stakeholders face in a crisis. For example, swift and effective evacuations following a chemical release can protect the lives and health of community members. Organizations need to protect physical, financial, and reputational assets during a crisis.

A crisis in one corporation can threaten an entire industry. An *E. coli* outbreak in Odwalla juices is an example. Odwalla is one of a handful of juice makers that did not pasteurize their juices. Their natural processes seek to retain the fruits' and vegetables' original nutrients. These companies have strict policies about their raw materials to safeguard against *E. coli* and other contaminants. The Odwalla crisis raised fears that not pasteurizing might be too dangerous. Odwalla shifted to a flash pasteurization process. If the government concluded all juice should be pasteurized, the non-pasteurized juice industry would be no more. The Food and Drug Administration (FDA) does not require juices to be pasteurized but warns people of the risk of exposure to the bacteria when they drink them.

Crisis management is "a set of factors designed to combat crises and to lessen the actual damage inflicted by a crisis."[7] Thinking of crisis management as a set of factors is at the heart of viewing crisis management as company DNA. Too many crisis managers think that simply having a crisis management plan is crisis management. Too often preparation is assessed by the question, "Do you have a crisis management plan?" A plan in a binder is not crisis management. A crisis management plan is not equivalent to being prepared. The crisis plan does nothing to help your organization combat crises on a day-to-day basis. A crisis management plan (CMP) in a binder is an add-on, something you have. Some companies may go a step further and perform media training, in which members of the organization are trained to handle media questions in crisis situations.

A CMP and media training are valuable. However, they are not ends, they are means to an end. The end is true prevention and preparation, crisis management as DNA. CMP and media training are merely steps in preparation. A CMP is simply a reference tool in a crisis, not a how-to guide. And a crisis team that believes a CMP tells them the exact steps to follow in a crisis is in for a rude awakening and their stakeholders are in for a rough ride. A CMP preassigns tasks and responsibilities, provides important contact information, and contains forms to help crisis team members record important information, such as stakeholder queries and what actions they have taken.[8] Media training may help your spokespeople deliver the crisis information and messages more effectively, but it does not collect the information or draft the messages to be sent. Neither a CMP nor media training contributes to mitigation. The best-managed crisis is the one that was avoided. CMPs and media training are like security blankets. Management feels better that they are there. But in reality, neither is sufficient to create effective crisis management.

To appreciate crisis management as DNA, it is helpful to consider the roots of crisis management. Crisis management evolved from emergency preparedness. Visit the Federal Emergency Management Agency (FEMA) Web site (www.fema.gov) and you will notice the similarities. FEMA requires all local areas to have emergency management plans. But FEMA does not equate a plan with preparation. Local emergency managers are required to regularly practice/exercise their plans. The type of exercise varies from sitting around the table discussing the crisis to in-the-field simulations with real people. Chapter 6 discusses the various exercise types. FEMA has a schedule for how often the various types of exercises should be performed. In addition, FEMA has local emergency managers engage in mitigation, their term for prevention. FEMA realizes that prevention is preferable to managing an emergency and that a plan is pointless unless it is tested through exercises. Hurricane Katrina highlighted the fact that FEMA, with its emphasis on preparation, can fail. No process is perfect in a crisis.

Crisis management as company DNA requires an ongoing commitment and execution of crisis management. Every organization needs a full-time crisis manager whose responsibilities include regularly collecting and assessing information about organizational risks. The crisis manager is trying to identify and then reduce crisis risks. The crisis manager is also responsible for keeping the CMP up to date and making sure there are regular crisis exercises. A CMP loses relevance as it sits on a shelf, because an organization evolves and those changes need to be reflected in the plan. For instance, the fact that people change jobs means that contacts and contact information changes. A CMP has no value until it is tested in an exercise. Only an exercise will help you determine if the CMP has the necessary and correct information and if the right people are on the crisis team.

OVERVIEW OF THE BOOK

Chapters 2, 3, and 4 identify the main types of crises organizations are likely to face. Cases are used to demonstrate the threat posed by the crises, identify ideas for detection and prevention, and illustrate effective and ineffective crisis responses. Each of these chapters provides a summary of what can be learned from the cases with a focus on the crisis response.

Chapter 5 is dedicated to the idea of a crisis-sensing network. The value of such a network is explained along with recommendations for creating one in your own organization. Chapter 6 returns to the idea of the CMP. The focus is on making the CMP a living document. The chapter also explains the value and variety in crisis exercises. Chapter 7 reviews the meaning of crisis management as organizational DNA. Recommendations are provided for how to move an organization from crisis management as an add-on to crisis management as DNA. The focus is on managing the organizational change necessary to make crisis management part of the organization's DNA.

I have tried to keep the book as jargon-free as possible. However, there is a language of crisis management. Table 1.1 provides a list of key crisis management terms and their definitions.

SUMMARY

In some ways, crisis management as an add-on may be more dangerous than no crisis preparation at all. If management thinks a CMP will protect them from harm, they are mistaken. CMPs do not actively seek to prevent crises, they help orchestrate responses to a crisis. If the plan is not updated or practiced, the crisis response will be ineffective and could even worsen the damage from the crisis. Crisis management as add-on creates a false sense of security that could lead to an ineffective or harmful crisis response.

Crisis management as DNA requires a true commitment. Top management must provide the resources and public commitment to crisis management. A crisis manager must routinely collect information that might contain risk information—engage in crisis sensing. Other departments in the organization need to respect and support the crisis management function by supplying the requested

TABLE 1.1:
KEY CRISIS MANAGEMENT TERMS

Accident Crisis: crisis that occurs because of technical-errors. The organization did not intend for the event to happen and/or could not control the event. The accident crisis category includes product harm, industrial accidents, transportation mishaps, challenges, and loss of key personnel.

Attack on Organization Crisis: crisis that occurs when some outside stakeholder or employee seeks to harm the organization in some way. The attack on organization crisis type includes product tampering, terrorism, rumors, workplace violence, and computer attacks.

Crisis: an unpredictable, major threat that can have a negative effect on the organization, industry, or stakeholders if handled improperly.

Crisis Management: a set of factors used to combat crises and to reduce the actual damage inflicted by a crisis.

Crisis Management Plan (CMP): a set of loose guidelines and forms that are used as a reference by the crisis team. It is sometimes called a crisis communication plan.

Crisis Management Team/Crisis Team: the people responsible for running crisis management effort and making key decisions.

Crisis Sensing Network: a mechanism for collecting and analyzing information about crisis risks. It is designed to funnel all possible crisis risk-related information to the crisis manager.

Crisis Types: the various categories of crises. Crises can be grouped into three types: attack on the organization, accident, and management misconduct.

Drill: an exercise that focuses on one element of crisis preparedness such as evacuation.

EOP: Emergency Operations Plan, a community plan for disasters that is similar to a CMP.

Exercise: a practice activity where people address a simulated crisis event.

Facilitator: a person who helps to develop, conduct, and evaluate a crisis exercise.

Federal Emergency Management Agency (FEMA): charged with preparing the U.S. for disasters and managing the federal response to disasters and recovery efforts. It is now part of the Department of Homeland Security.

Functional Exercise: an exercise that uses the Crisis Control Center and simulates interaction with emergency responders and other outsiders involved in the crisis. Does not involve the movement of real equipment or actions taken in the field.

Full-Scale Exercise: the most elaborate exercise where real actions are taken and the crisis team interacts with actual emergency responders and simulated crisis victims.

Incident: an occurrence of a crisis. Incident Management is often used synonymously with Crisis Management.

Instructing Information: information stakeholders need to know to protect themselves physically from a crisis such as shelter-in-place.

Hazmat: short hand for hazardous materials.

Management Misconduct Crisis: crisis created by management knowingly placing stakeholders at risk or purposefully violating laws or regulations. The management misconduct crisis type includes known risk, improper job performance, and purposeful legal/regulatory violation.

Mitigation: refers to efforts to prevent a crisis from occurring.

National Incident Management System (NIMS): the federal standard for the incident command structure to be used during disasters and crises. The idea is that all agencies will integrate more effectively if they all share an incident command structure. The use of NIMS is mandated by the Department of Homeland Security.

Orientation Seminar: an exercise where crisis team members learn about the CMP, their roles, and their responsibilities in a crisis.

Shelter-in-Place: when people are asked to stay inside and seal a building from outside air.

Stakeholder: anyone with an interest, or "stake," in the organization; stakeholder groups include employees and their families, customers, shareholders, directors, financial institutions, suppliers, distributors, government institutions (federal, state, and local), the media, and the communities in which an organization conducts business.

Tabletop Exercise: an exercise where members of the crisis team talk through a crisis situation.

information. The crisis manager also keeps the CMP current and makes sure there are regular drills to test the plan and the organization's level of preparedness. To maximize effectiveness, crisis management needs to be a part of your organization, embedded in the organization's DNA.

I

TYPES OF CRISES

2

Attacks on Organizations

In early 2005, there were high-profile security breaches at Choice-Point and George Washington University. At ChoicePoint, the personal information of over 145,000 people in the United States might have been compromised. Hackers harvested 30,000 names, Social Security numbers, and other data from the student and faculty files at George Washington University.[1] The reality is that most attacks on corporate computer systems are performed by disgruntled employees, not outside hackers. Organizations are targets for attacks, both internal and external, in cyberspace and physical space. Attacks are premeditated actions designed to harm the organization and/or its personnel. Attacks also create collateral damage for stakeholders. Just ask the people whose identity information was lost at ChoicePoint and George Washington University if they are worried about identity theft.

Attacks on organizations take a variety of forms. All harm an organization reputationally and financially. The worst attacks result in loss of life of employees and/or external stakeholders. Product tampering, workplace violence, and terrorism fall on the extreme side because there is potential for loss of life. Computer hacking/tampering and rumors are less extreme but can be costly for an organization and its stakeholders. Attacks are intentional actions taken by people working against the organization. There is no perfect defense against any of these attacks. All organizations are vulnerable in some fashion.

COMPUTER HACKING/TAMPERING

In today's wired world, computers and the Internet are indispensable. They are also a significant source of vulnerability. Outsiders can hack into a system or shut a system down through denial of service. Insiders can damage a system as well. Let's consider some examples of the different variations of computer hacking/tampering.

Online companies such as Amazon.com and eBay live by Internet sales. Yahoo! makes money by people visiting its Web sites. What happens when customers cannot access their Web sites? Lost customers equals lost revenue. Hackers use a procedure called denial of service to block access to Web sites. This causes the Web site to be overloaded with traffic, so there is no hacking. Routers are overloaded with so much fake traffic that real customers cannot access the site. Denial of service attacks require very little computer skills. Ironically, you can download programs for denial of service attacks from the Internet.[2] A set of attacks in February 2000 resulted in a estimated $100 million in lost revenues for various Internet companies. Among those affected were eBay for ninety minutes, Amazon for one hour, Yahoo! for three hours, and e-Trade for ninety minutes. The source of the attack? A fifteen-year-old Canadian hacker.[3] Denial of service is a federal crime in the United States. The FBI handled the 2000 cases. Denial of service can cost organizations and investors money.

Computer Hacking Case: ChoicePoint

ChoicePoint is a data brokering firm. Their databases include Social Security numbers, credit and medical histories, motor vehicle registration, job applications, lawsuits, criminal files, and other sensitive information. The database has over 19 billion entries. The thieves created false accounts by posing as clients of ChoicePoint. It is known that 35,000 people had their detailed information taken.

A total of 110,000 people were sent letters warning them that their information may have been compromised. Police only learned about the case because California law requires a company to notify people about security breaches that could compromise their identities. Very few states have such notification laws. Authorities estimate that up to 500,000 people could be at risk. The thieves used fax machines at a Kinko's office to run the scam. One arrest has been made so far.[4] In 2004, hackers breached a computer at the University of California at Berkeley and harvested information from 1.4 million personnel records of state in-home care receivers.[5] Hacking can place customers at risk for identity theft.

Hacking/tampering can be a result of insider attacks. A study sponsored by the U.S. Department of Homeland Security found that most insider attacks are committed by employees seeking revenge against their bosses. Employees might be angry over a disciplinary action, missed promotion, or a layoff, for example. In one case an employee unhappy with his severance package caused a company's communication system to go down for two days. In addition to crippling networks, insider attacks might delete critical software. Whatever the nature of the attack, the organization takes a financial loss.[6]

But should we really worry about computer hacking/tampering? Yes. Studies show that about 90 percent of all corporations detected at least one computer security breach per year. The FBI estimates that only about 34 percent of such crimes are ever reported. Corporations fear the negative publicity.[7] Your company and your stakeholders are at risk.

Prevention and Detection

The Pentagon contends with hundreds of computer attacks each day. The good news is they have a high success rate in defeating the attacks. The bad news is that your organization is probably not the Pentagon. You probably have some sort of firewall to protect your computer. Though that is good, it is not enough to protect your organization. Security experts recommend a range of intrusion detection devices and software and even countermeasures. The devices and software warn an organization of an attack, an attempt to breach security, or a denial of service. There are aggressive programs that respond in kind to denial of service attacks. Your company needs to decide what is right for its goals.

There are two steps that are critical to prevention of computer hacking/tampering. The first is a thorough analysis of your computer-based vulnerabilities. Where are you vulnerable? What types of equipment, software, security, protocols, and training can help address those vulnerabilities? Internal threats are best prevented through proper security clearance, including biometrics, and encryption. A worker who has been laid off should not be able to reenter the facility or the computer system. Experts note that there are warning signs for inside saboteurs. The warning signs include tardiness, missing work, and arguing with co-workers. Management should monitor employees facing disciplinary action and provide formal grievance procedures for those who feel wronged.[8] Make sure only the authorized personnel have complete access and the ability to revoke access if an employee appears to be a problem. Also, it is important to train people so they know the proper security protocols and do not accidentally give vital information away or allow people into your system by loaning them their computer ID.

Basic Crisis Response

The response to computer hacking/tampering is delicate. Why announce a problem when you don't have to? That logic has limited applications. First, other states are following California's lead and requiring companies to contact stakeholders when their identity information may have been compromised. It takes an average of three years to recover from identity theft.[9] It is good customer service to warn the people that they have been placed at risk. It is also the basic crisis response. Your first message should tell people what to do to protect themselves from the crisis. If stakeholder identities are at risk, send them a letter of notification that includes the steps they should take. Second, the FBI has special InfraGard chapters that keep investigations private. The news media will not find and publish a police report. The FBI can help your organization fix the problem without publicity.

If the crime goes public, explain what preventive measures were in place prior to the incident, note what is being done to solve the crime, and indicate general changes designed to prevent a repeat of the crisis. You may or may not want to talk about future preventive actions. Security is best kept private so you can just note that changes will be made without providing details. Remember that your company is a victim, too. It's all right to acknowledge that.

RUMORS

Rumors are untrue information about your organization that are circulating publicly. The key points here are *untrue* and *public*. Bad news about your company that is true is not a rumor. Someone expressing a negative opinion about your organization, product, or service is not a rumor. The Internet has facilitated the ability to spread rumors. With millions of people posting and e-mailing millions of messages each day, cyberspace is fertile ground for rumors. Visit either www.snopes.com or www.truthorfiction.com to separate Internet fact from fiction. Both sites are dedicated to debunking rumors.

Rumor Case: The Infamous Tommy Hilfiger Comment

In 1996, the Internet was abuzz with the Oprah–Tommy Hilfiger showdown. Messages about the conflict were sent via e-mail and posted at various discussion groups. A sample message is provided in Exhibit 2.1. The basic story is that clothing designer Tommy Hilfiger appeared as a guest on the *Oprah Winfrey Show*. She asked him if it was true that he did not like having African Americans, Hispanics, and Asians wearing his clothes. He said "yes" and that he wished those people would not wear his clothes because they were not made for them. Oprah then threw him off of her show.

> *Exhibit 2.1*
> Subject: FWD: Tommy Hilfiger hates us . . .
> Did you see the recent Oprah Winfrey show on which Tommy Hilfiger was a guest? Oprah asked Hilfiger if his alleged statements about people of color were true—he's been accused of saying things such as "If I had known that African-Americans, Hispanics and Asians would buy my clothes, I would not have made them so nice," and "I wish those people would not buy my clothes—they were made for upper-class whites." What did he say when Oprah asked him if he said these things? He said "Yes." Oprah immediately asked Hilfiger to leave her show.
> Now, let's give Hilfiger what he's asked for—let's not buy his clothes. Boycott! Please—pass this message along.

Tommy Hilfiger has never appeared on the *Oprah Winfrey Show*, nor has he ever made such statements. In fact, Hilfiger ads feature a diverse group of models. The rumor was untrue, but the e-mails and the postings calling for boycotts (the threat) were real. Hilfiger could have lost customers because of the rumor and did suffer reputational damage. Who wants to be known as a racist? The company used the Internet to respond to the rumor. Responses from the company were posted at discussion groups where the rumor was being talked about. A section of the company's own Web site was dedicated to the rumor, www.tommy.com/about/about_us.aspy?cat=Rumor. Exhibit 2.2 lists comments from the site, including one from Tommy Hilfiger and one from Oprah Winfrey. You can also find refutations at the two rumor debunking sites noted earlier.

Exhibit 2.2

Tommy Hilfiger: "I am deeply upset that a malicious and completely false rumor continues to circulate about me. I create my clothing for all different types of people regardless of their race, religious or cultural background. I want you to know the facts so that you are not the victim of a classic 'urban myth' that perpetuates untruths and has no basis in reality. Please read further to learn the truth."

Oprah Winfrey: "So I want to just set the record straight once and for all. The rumor claims that clothing designer Tommy Hilfiger came on this show and made racist remarks, and that I then kicked him out. I just want to say that is not true because it just never happened.

"Tommy Hilfiger has never appeared on this show. READ MY LIPS, TOMMY HILFIGER HAS NEVER APPEARED ON THIS SHOW. And all of [the] people who claim that they saw it, they heard it—it never happened. I've never even met Tommy Hilfiger."

Taped live on *The Oprah Winfrey Show*, January 11, 1999

The rumor originated in a Philippines tabloid newspaper. The original story claimed Hilfiger had said he had not made the clothes for Filipinos and wished they would stop wearing them. A variation has the incident occurring on *CNN Style* with designer Elsa Klensch. A nearly identical rumor spread about Liz Claiborne in 1991.

But these are rumors, right? "Sticks and stones will break my bones but words will never hurt me." Experts disagree. Don Middleberg, a pioneer in cyber–public relations, observes, "A lot of stuff [statements in cyberspace] is malicious. If companies let these rumors fester without responding to them, they can get hurt."[10] Rumors damage reputations and ultimately inflict financial damage if the reputation is damaged enough.

Prevention and Detection

Clearly we cannot prevent a rumor. People will create messages and place them in cyberspace. Other people will find the messages interesting and believable and relay them. That is human nature—rumors have spread for thousands of years without the Internet. In the 1980s, a popular rumor was that the candy Pop Rocks would explode in your stomach if you ate them and then drank a soda. Now it is easier to reach more people and faster. Prevention in this case means preventing or limiting damage and that is keyed to detection.

Detection involves a close monitoring of the Internet. Easier said then done, you might protest. The Internet is composed of millions of Web pages, discussion postings, and web logs or blogs. The good news and bad news is that these messages are public. You can find them, but so can your stakeholders. Companies such as CyberAlert (www.cyberalert.com) and eWatch (www.ewatch.com), specialize in monitoring all facets of the Internet for statements about your organization. For a fee, they will monitor, collect, and analyze Internet comments about your organization. They will perform the standard searches of the Internet news media as well as print, radio, and television. By casting a wide net you can identify rumors early.

Basic Crisis Response

The old logic for rumors was to ignore them and they would fade away. As Middleberg suggests, the best response now is take the offensive. Messages have a long life and potential reach on the Internet. The response to a rumor should follow the two-pronged approach of Tommy Hilfiger. First, post replies to sites on the Internet where the rumors are found. Make it clear you represent the organization in question. Provide evidence to support your claim and links to additional sites for further information. Second, dedicate part of your Web site to refuting the rumor. Provide evidence, including testimonials, that debunk the rumor. Tommy Hilfiger's site included a testimonial from Oprah herself. You can even provide links to other sites that support you. The Hilfiger site featured links to the rumor on both the snopes.com and truthorfiction.com Web sites. When Febreze faced rumors that its product could kill pets, it provided links to the page at http://urbanlegends.about.com, another rumor-debunking site. Crisis managers need to deny and attack the accusers. Deny that a crisis exists and attack those who would lie about your organization.

PRODUCT TAMPERING

Product tampering is when an individual or group alters a product to cause harm or for financial gain. Tampering can kill people. People have died from tampered-with Sudafed and Tylenol. People may tamper to extort money from a company, to cause random harm, or to cover a crime. The Sudafed tampering was done to try to cover the murder of a spouse. Other times people will seek money. Enter the strange case of Wendy's and the fingertip.

Product Tampering Case: Wendy's Fingertip

In March 2005 Americans were horrified with Anna Ayala's tale of biting on a 1.5-inch piece of fingertip while dining on Wendy's chili in San José. It was like an episode of a TV crime show. Whose fingertip was it? Did it belong to an employee or someone who supplied Wendy's with ingredients for the chili? Was it in the chili before or after it was cooked? The fingertip was fingerprinted and run through law enforcement databases and its DNA analyzed. The fingertip was autopsied. The autopsy determined the fingertip had not been cooked, suggesting the suspicion of tampering. Wendy's offered a $10,000 reward to match a person to the fingertip. In May the fingertip was traced to a co-worker of Ayala's husband. She was arrested for her crime, product tampering. The pair pled guilty to charges of attempted grand theft and conspiring to make a false claim in September 2005. Wendy's, meanwhile, lost millions of dollars in depressed sales in northern California and reputational damage for the nearly two-month fingertip coverage.[11]

Product tampering results in drop in sales, lost revenues, and costs associated with any recalls or lawsuits stemming from the tampering. It can also result in injuries or death. Tampering is a threat to any organization that creates something customers consume or place on their bodies. We are particularly vulnerable to food, drinks, medicines, vitamins, herbal supplements, and any skin care products. Tampered products can cause harm when ingested or placed in contact with the skin. Organizations and their stake-holders are placed at risk by tampering.

Prevention and Detection

If you notice, the package on many products says "tamper resis-tant," not "tamper proof." *Tamper proof* indicates there is no risk. If only tampering was 100 percent preventable! We have plastic rings on soft drinks, covers on jars of peanut butter, and seals on medicine bottles. If we see the seals are broken, we know not to eat, drink, or use the product. Tamper-resistant packaging is the best line of prevention. Even so, a clever and determined perpetrator will find a way to tamper with a product, or an unsuspecting consumer may miss the warning signs.

Organizations must closely monitor reports of product harm, cases where people are injured by a product. These cases must be evaluated seriously to determine if the tampering is real or fake. This means making it easy for customers to report prob-lems and concerns. Web sites and toll-free numbers on prod-ucts make it easier for customers to let you know when there is a problem.

Basic Crisis Response

How an organization responds depends on the results of its inves-tigation. If the tampering was a hoax designed to extort money, the organization treats it much like a rumor. The organization provides the evidence to show it was not at fault and any evidence that the event might be a result of tampering. A beer company once autop-sied a mouse to prove it was forced into a bottle by the customer and did not drown by being bottled in the beer. The fingertip autopsy was critical to Wendy's case. If the fingertip had not been cooked, odds are someone other than an employee or supply chain member was responsible for it being there. Prove your denial and prosecute those involved in the crime.

When there is a problem, the organization must recall the prod-uct and warn customers not to use it. It is not pleasant to have to tell customers your product might harm them. Be sure to note that tampering—a criminal act—and not actions of your organization lead to the recall. The organization is victim of product tampering just like the customers.

WORKPLACE VIOLENCE

Workplace violence is when someone in the workplace is the victim of a violent act, whether random, from a familiar contact (e.g., an enraged spouse), or from a current or former employee. In the case of disgruntled workers, many resort to physical violence, as opposed to computer sabotage or other nonphysical methods of revenge. Dramatic examples involve multiple shootings. One of the first workplace violence incidents to receive widespread attention was at the U.S. Post Office in Royal Oak, Michigan, in which Tom McIlvane opened fire on November 14, 1991, after losing an arbitration hearing, killing four and wounding five others before taking his own life. Since then the U.S. Postal Service has worked hard to reduce incidents of workplace violence and the problem has spread to other companies.

Workplace Violence Case: Nu-Wood Decorative Mill

The Nu-Wood Decorative Mill plant erupted in violence in July 2001. An employee shot and killed a co-worker and injured six others.[12] The plant is located in Goshen, Indiana, a town of about 29,000 people. Workplace violence happens in big and small towns and in white-collar and blue-collar facilities. Any organization that has employees is vulnerable to workplace violence. The violence can be triggered by events at work, such as layoffs or discipline, or by events at home, such as divorce or a child custody battle. The crises are sudden, violent, and tragic.

Prevention and Detection

It would be nice if workplace violence were easy to predict, but it isn't. Organizations can conduct thorough background checks, deny reentry to former employees, and monitor public spaces for signs of violence as preventive measures. Reentry is a major issue. For example, Jack comes back to the main gate he has used for years. He says he left something in his locker, so security lets him through. His pass still works, so he enters the facility with a loaded gun. Any fired or laid-off workers should be escorted from the premises by security personnel. No former employee should reenter a facility. All codes or locks must be changed to prevent reentry.

Current employees, as in the Nu-Wood case, can be the threat. There are limited detection options for workplace violence. The warning signs are the same as for sabotage: tardiness, missing work, and arguing with co-workers. These signs may suggest that the employee is worth watching, though not necessarily that he or she will become violent. In most cases it is a younger male who engages in workplace violence. We can add threats of violence and verbal aggression to the list of concerns. These last two concerns demand investigation and may result in dismissal if the employee violated workplace violence policies. Threats and verbal aggression are serious warning signs that must be reported to management. Employees may be reluctant to do so because a person could be fired for those actions. Encourage workers to report the warning signs. Moreover, train management to identify the warning signs. Many companies offer seminars in workplace violence detection. In one organization a worker had "psycho" on the nametag of his work jacket. The worker often said he might "get people" in the organization some day. One day he did. Was there a warning sign there?

Basic Crisis Response

The response to workplace violence should focus on helping the victims. Clearly state your concern for the victims and their families. Discuss what is being done to help the injured and the families of those hurt or killed. When there was a shooting at the Lockheed Martin plant in Meridian, Mississippi, the company response started, "We are shocked and saddened by this tragedy and express our deepest sympathies to the families."[13] This response can include covering medical costs and providing psychological counseling. Emphasize this is a tragedy for everyone involved, including the management of the facility. All employees at the organization suffer the effects of the violence.

TERRORISM

Terrorism involves the use of violence or threat of violence against people or property to create fear or intimidation to achieve some objective. Terrorism is not new to global companies. They have dealt with the problem for years. However, terrorism is relatively new on U.S. soil. The horrific events of September 11, 2001, reinforced that terrorism was no longer merely a problem "over there." The Oklahoma City and first World Trade Center bombings were earlier warnings that terrorism had arrived in the United States. Terrorism was occurring in our own back yard. Organizations are terrorist targets if they manufacture or utilize hazardous materials (chemical, biological, or radiological), are vital to defense or economic infrastructure, are involved in transportation, or are located near a target including historic areas and government offices. Terrorism can be a threat to a wide array of organizations. The damage can be severe with loss of life, property, and financial assets.

Terrorism Case: World Trade Center, 1993

For $300, Yousef created a bomb he thought would bring down Tower One of the World Trade Center and send a poison cloud into the air. On February 26, 1993, he detonated his 1,300-pound bomb in an underground parking garage. The result was 6 people killed and another 1,040 injured. This was a tragedy, but not on the scale Yousef envisioned. The explosion vaporized his poison, so it was not a factor. Tower One did not collapse; only the first six floors were damaged. The economic toll was in the hundreds of millions. Tower One reopened on April 1 following the reopening of Tower Two on March 26.

At the time of the blast, over 900 businesses had operations in the World Trade Center (WTC). Closing the WTC meant they had no place to conduct business and limited opportunities to reenter the building and collect valuable data and equipment. The blast occurred on a Friday. On the following Monday, only 10 of those 900 companies were operating as usual. One of those was Fiduciary Trust International. They activated their business continuity plan and had a fully equipped alternate site, called a hot site, up and running by Monday morning.[14]

Prevention and Detection

No surprise that post–September 11 corporate spending on security has increased. External security is the primary preventive for terrorism. The focus is on control of access through perimeter security and building access. Organizations try to keep potential terrorists away from their property and out of their buildings. Even though they have been criticized for lack of security, many in the chemical industry have made it more difficult for people to get near or into a facility. Detection centers on observation. Cameras, software, and human eyes scan the external perimeter and inside of facilities for suspicious activities. Everyone in an organization must watch for suspicious people, packages, and vehicles. Terrorism is a human threat, and those are the most difficult kinds to monitor. People try to hide their activities. These are similar to the recommendations organizations use for workplace violence.

Basic Crisis Response

The first priority in a response is to warn stakeholders if the terrorist event has placed them at risk. Is there a danger from a chemical release? Is there contamination to the food or water supply? Tell stakeholders what the threat is and how best to protect themselves from it. Express concern for those harmed by the attack and their families. Terrorism will result in injuries and deaths, possibly on a grand scale such as Oklahoma City and September 11. Finally, note that the organization is a victim of the terrorism attack as well and how the group is trying to recover. If possible, provide a timeline indicating when the organization will be operational again and what you are doing to help customers until operations resume. During this time the organization should work to contain the damage, limit the threat, and provide aid to victims.

SUMMARY: WHAT WE KNOW ABOUT ATTACKS ON ORGANIZATIONS

A feature of attacks on organizations is that the organization itself can be a victim. The organization might be a victim along with injured stakeholders (product tampering, terrorism, workplace violence, and some hacking) or alone (some hacking and rumors). Johnson & Johnson pioneered the victim-oriented response during the first Tylenol product tampering event in 1982. Reminding people of your victim status helps build sympathy for the organization. People naturally attribute the cause to factors the organization could not control, so stakeholders are predisposed to respond favorably to the victim message.

The key is to make the victim theme a visible but minor part of the response. The first priority are the stakeholders. Express sympathy for those affected, including the families. Warn stakeholders if they are at risk and what actions they need to take to protect themselves.

Telling people their identity is at risk is not pleasant. But warning them and outlining actions they should take to lessen the risk is better than hiding in silence. Customers appreciate warnings and advice more than the surprise of discovering identity theft on their own. Be stakeholder-centric with your response while including your role as victim. This response will help protect your reputation and preserve the relationships with stakeholders.

3

When Things Go Bad

We've all had days when nothing seems to go right. The car won't start. The computer shuts down, erasing an important file. There is an accident on the drive home and a twenty-minute ride turns into a two-hour wait. Call it bad luck or accidents, but bad things do happen, even to good people. The same holds true for organizations. Your organization can follow all the safety rules, complete all the preventive maintenance, and perform all the safety checks, but things happen. Dust particles ignite and explode, new evidence suggests a prescription drug is unsafe, an airplane crashes, the CEO has an unexpected health crisis, or an activist group claims you are acting immorally.

All of the crises noted at the start of this chapter are accidental in nature. Your organization did not intend to cause and/or could not control the circumstances that led to the problem. The organization is a victim of circumstance. Accidental crises are a little harder to manage because the organization is held somewhat accountable for them. Stakeholders attribute a moderate amount of responsibility for the crisis to your organization.[1] There are five types of accident crises: (1) product harm, (2) industrial accidents, (3) transportation mishaps, (4) challenges (e.g., charges of unethical conduct), and (5) sudden loss of key personnel.

TECHNICAL ERROR PRODUCT HARM

A product harm crisis occurs when a product you make is found to be a threat to stakeholders. Contaminated food, defective mechanical parts, or adverse reactions to medications are examples. To be viewed as accidental, the product harm must be a technical error. A *technical error* means the product harm was a result of unforeseen circumstances. You did not know the harm would occur, and danger was somehow undetectable. The harm was not a result of people failing to do their jobs.

Product Harm Case: Chi-Chi's Hepatitis A

If you've ever eaten in a Mexican restaurant, you know that green onions are a common ingredient. Frequently they are eaten raw. This tasty vegetable was a knockout blow to Chi-Chi's, a restaurant chain already in bankruptcy under Chapter 11 protection. In fall 2003, people eating and working at a Chi-Chi's restaurant in the Beaver Valley Mall, twenty-five miles northwest of Pittsburgh, were exposed to hepatitis A by the green onions. As a result of the exposure, 3 people died and another 640 people were sickened. Following the incident, Chi-Chi's restaurants in the area were ghost towns. At first the fear was that Chi-Chi's was to blame by allowing an infected worker to spread the deadly disease. State health officials and the U.S. Food and Drug Administration (FDA) proved that the green onions were the source. Chi-Chi's immediately removed green onions from its food and cooperated fully in the investigation. The health officials noted that Chi-Chi's was helpless in the situation. Once the contaminated onions entered the restaurant, there was nothing Chi-Chi's could have done to prevent the outbreak.[2]

The state of Pennsylvania took the lead by providing hepatitis vaccines to worried stakeholders. Due to constraints from the bankruptcy, Chi-Chi's slowly began to pay people for medical expenses. The initial agreement by the bankruptcy judge was for Chi-Chi's to pay lost wages and out-of-pocket medical expenses of between $3,000 and $20,000. Any claims over $20,000 would have to be approved by the bankruptcy court. Chi-Chi's was criticized for this slow response on medical bills but had no choice in the matter.[3] The weakened chain itself could not survive the damage done by the hepatitis A outbreak.

Product Harm Case: Pfizer and Viagra

Pfizer is a major pharmaceutical company that produces a number of well-known medications. Their most popular medication by far is Viagra. Since being introduced in 1998, over 23 million men worldwide have taken Viagra. In 2004 Pfizer sales topped $1.6 billion for Viagra. In May 2005, seven years after its introduction, the news media began reporting on a study that suggests that Viagra can cause blindness. The FDA had 38 reports of blindness by Viagra users. The specific type of blindness is called nonarteritic anterior ischemic optic neuropathy or NAION. It is a common form of nerve damage experienced by people over the age of fifty. NAION does occur in men with high cholesterol, diabetes, or high blood pressure. Oddly these are the same risk factors of impotence.

Pfizer has always included a warning on the Viagra label stating that it could affect eyesight. A smaller number of cases have been reported by users of Cialis, Eli Lilly & Co.'s male impotence medication. Obviously this is a cause for concern. People worry when blindness is a side effect. That is much different than backaches or nausea. Pfizer promised to work with the FDA to investigate the situation further. Pfizer noted that "there is no evidence that NAION occurred more frequently in men taking Viagra than men of similar age and health who did not take Viagra." Although there was no recall, people learned of a possible new harmful side effect from Viagra. The FDA continued to investigate the case. From the outset, Pfizer was willing to add to the Viagra warning label that it could, in rare cases, cause blindness. However, that change would not be made until there was proof of a link between Viagra and NAION.[4]

The news was not as good for Merck, when reports surfaced that its anti-inflammatory drug Vioxx was linked to increased risk of heart disease. In fall 2004, Merck researchers noted some troubling findings in a study designed to test Vioxx as a preventive in the recurrence of colon cancer. The three-year study involved over 2,000 patients. The disturbing result was that those taking the high doses of Vioxx showed an increased risk of cardiovascular events compared with those who were not taking the drug. In plain English, those taking Vioxx had a greater number of heart attacks and strokes than those who weren't taking it.[5] This was a serious threat to patients and to Merck. Sales of Vioxx generated $2.5 billion for Merck in 2004. Merck recalled Vioxx and watched as its stock price plummeted.[6]

Merck's situation was complicated by reports that it had known of the health risk since 2000. British medical weekly *The Lancet* claimed that Vioxx should have been pulled from the market four years earlier because there was sufficient evidence then linking the arthritis drug to an increased risk of strokes and heart attacks. The journal strongly criticized the U.S. drug company for failing to stop marketing the drug in 2000 when data showed that Vioxx was potentially dangerous. "The licensing of Vioxx and its continued use in the face of unambiguous evidence of harm have been public health catastrophes," editor Richard Horton said in a commentary. "This controversy will not end with the drug's withdrawal." U.S. pharmaceutical giant Merck disputed the claim made by *The Lancet* that Vioxx should have been pulled from the market earlier. Merck said it posted a scientific critique on its Web site "to further clarify for the scientific community why Merck disagrees with the conclusions" of *The Lancet*. The statement said the scientific critique details why Merck disagrees with analysis published in *The Lancet* and added that until a study this year, "data from Merck's clinical trials showed no significant difference in cardiovascular risk" from taking Vioxx. Merck claimed that "it was vigilant in monitoring and disclosing the cardiovascular safety" of Vioxx and added that the company "absolutely disagrees with any implication to the contrary."

The debate centered over how the data were collected. The early studies suggesting Vioxx was linked to cardiovascular problems were based on observational data, not experimental data. Physicians were looking back to see if patients had more cardiovascular episodes than those taking other arthritis medication. The numbers seemed to be higher in the Vioxx users. Merck maintained that this did not prove a link. Their point was that there could have been other factors contributing to the higher rate. Merck contended that only clinical trials can account for these differences and can be trusted.[7] Their data provided such a clinical trial, and the drug was pulled from the market. Merck might have been damaged by this debate over methods. The company did wait for the research and data, but most consumers do not fully understand or appreciate the difference between observational studies and clinical (experimental) studies.

Prevention and Detection

Technical error product harm instances are tough to prevent. Following all inspection and safety protocols is the best prevention. This means thorough testing of product quality and safety and following all guidelines for safe manufacturing and product handling. As the Viagra, Vioxx, and Chi-Chi's cases illustrate, technical error product harm can lurk unseen. Suddenly the risk manifests itself with little warning. The organization then relies on detection. Organizations need to carefully monitor customer complaints by paying very close attention to those reporting harm or illness. You are looking for patterns, a number of people experiencing the same problem. The first step is to investigate. Are these claims real or is someone trying to make money à la the Wendy's fingertip (see chapter 2). Legitimate cases require your organization to take action.

The Vioxx case is the only one to have detection issues. True, observational studies are not the same as clinical studies for assessing risks. But the observational data suggest a potential problem. In fact, Merck did modify label warnings previously to note the cardiovascular risk. Some people may think that they should have acted sooner. The court cases may prove them right. Thus far the court decisions on Vioxx have been split with Merck losing the first case and winning the second. There are still over 7,000 cases to be tried. But Merck followed accepted procedures for testing the safety of Vioxx and acted quickly once it had the appropriate clinical data. However, not all people and juries will view Merck as responsible. Some advocates feel that pharmaceutical testing in general needs to be reformed to be more sensitive to risks to improve detection. That is a debate that will rage on in Washington, D.C.

Basic Crisis Response

Your customers are the top priority because they can suffer from technical error product harm. Warn customers of the danger and what they can do to protect themselves from the product. This means identifying the exact product that could cause harm. In food recalls, it is common to give batch numbers. If you can isolate when the problem occurred, you know the batches affected and unaffected by the threat. If it is a recall, tell customers how to return the product and/or dispose of it safely.

NESCO/American Harvest exemplifies the ideal recall response in their handling of their 2003 recall of a deep fryer. The recall was limited to specific models: DF-250T, DF-1250T, and DF-1250TL. The models were noted in the news release and on their Web site. In addition, NESCO/American Harvest helped people visually identify the models. The models in question did not have writing on the cover that said "Attention: Remove lid when frying French fries and high moisture food. Ensure both the lid and tank are completely dry after washing and before use." Pictures on the Web site showed where to look for the warning. Customers were told to stop using the recalled fryers immediately. On their Web site was a link that allowed customers to complete a form related to the recall. By completing the form, a customer would be sent a new lid with the warning and a free gift. The warning was necessary because water in the cover can drain into the oil reservoir, causing a boilover of the oil and risk of burns. At the time of the recall, 47,000 deep fryers had covers without warnings and the company had received 7 reports of hot oil spills.[8]

If there is no recall, tell people what is being done to minimize the risk. This can involve changing labels (an option for Viagra) or identifying the source of the threat and how it was removed (Chi-Chi's removing the green onions).

Express concern for those injured and those at risk. Merck provides an example of a company attempting to show concern in the face of mounting public pressure and looming court cases. In the recall announcement, Merck president and chief executive officer Raymond V. Gilmartin stated: "We are taking this action because we believe it best serves the interests of patients. Although we believe it would have been possible to continue to market Vioxx with labeling that would incorporate these new data, given the availability of alternative therapies, and the questions raised by the data, we concluded that a voluntary withdrawal is the responsible course to take." Merck took a very costly, voluntary action to help protect its customers. In fact, Merck itself discovered the problem while conducting additional product testing and informed the government.

Chi-Chi's chief operating officer, Bill Zavertnik, rang a note of concern as well.

> Chi-Chi's deeply regrets the recent spread of Hepatitis A in the Beaver Valley area of Pennsylvania. Over the years, our Company has developed and enacted food safety programs

that place the Company in the top percentile of national restaurant chains in the promotion and enforcement of the
highest standards of health and hygiene. Our hearts go out to
the families that have been impacted. . . . We sincerely apologize
to all of our loyal customers and want to inform the community
that Chi-Chi's will do everything within our power to make sure
that our patrons continue to enjoy a healthful and rewarding
dining experience and that our employees have a safe and
sanitized working atmosphere.[9]

The Chi-Chi's response expresses direct and indirect concern. The
direct concern is the regret and concern for those affected. The indirect concern is everything Chi-Chi's does to making dining safe.
Chi-Chi's is always thinking about customers by trying to keep
them safe.

You need to back up those words with actions as well. Pay for any
medical expenses caused by your product and cover the costs of
returning and replacing items. Chi-Chi's was criticized for a delay in
paying medical bills. The company was in bankruptcy and had to
gain a judge's approval before making any payments. Your insurance will help cover most of the costs, but there will be some
financial burden to bear.

Chi-Chi's added an additional element to its response by reinforcing that it was a technical error. Zavertnik also stated, "The
public health authorities confirmed that there was no possible way
that Chi-Chi's could have prevented this incident. There is currently
no industry-accepted means of testing produce for the Hepatitis A
virus. And beyond that, there is no way to wash Hepatitis A off
of contaminated green onions."[10] The statement reinforced that the
risk was something Chi-Chi's could not reasonably have detected or
prevented. This was critical because Chi-Chi's could have been to
blame. If there is doubt about the cause, be sure to reinforce that the
incident was a technical error beyond your control.

TECHNICAL ERROR INDUSTRIAL ACCIDENTS

Accidents, like product harm, can be the result of technical error
or human error. Technical errors are those beyond the reasonable control of the organization. The threat is hidden from normal
detection. The organization did not mean for the incident to occur,

it just did. Industrial accidents can include fires, explosions, and chemical releases. These crises place workers and community members at risk. For example, community members are at risk of exposure to hazardous chemicals an industrial accident might produce.

Industrial Accident Case: West Pharmaceuticals

The West Pharmaceuticals Rouse Road facility in Kinston, North Carolina, disappeared in a blast on January 29, 2003. The explosion killed six employees and damaged nearby buildings, and some people had to be evacuated. The facility manufactured intravenous fitments and syringe plungers. West Pharmaceuticals pledged to and did rebuild the facility a few miles away. The accident was investigated by the U.S. Chemical Safety Board (CSB), who led the investigation of the incident. The CSB is responsible for investigating the cause of major chemical accidents in the United States. The CSB quickly identified that the explosion was caused by a dust ignition. Employees used powdered rubber to produce the syringes and fitments. The organic rubber dust was identified as the fuel for the explosion. The CSB believes the rubber dust built up in the suspended ceiling in the processing area. The dust could have entered the ceiling through small openings in the ceiling of the air conditioning system.[11]

Organic dust is volatile and a common business risk. Oddly, there are few regulations governing organic dust. West Pharmaceuticals had performed the proper maintenance and followed the regulations. Dust had accumulated out of sight and then ignited. A spark as small as a static electrical charge can trigger a dust explosion (Preliminary Findings, 2003).

Prevention and Detection

The technical error aspect of industrial accidents make them difficult to detect and to prevent. Unseen dust in the ceiling destroyed an entire production facility! Detection and prevention occur after the fact. We learn from the accident what to look for next time and what action to take to prevent a repeat. The CSB, for instance, is urging stronger standards for organic dust. Organizations can learn from the CSB report how to prevent organic dust explosions and how to detect the threat.

Basic Crisis Response

The first step in an industrial accident response is providing instructional information. Stakeholders need to be told how to protect themselves from the physical threat of the crisis. West Pharmaceuticals evacuated a nearby school, informed people there was no environmental threat, and announced a special phone number and provided forms on its Web site to process insurance claims for shattered windows. Employees were told they would be relocated to its Kearney, Nebraska, facility until the new North Carolina facility was completed. The workers worked for three weeks, then returned home for one week in a rotating schedule. West Pharmaceuticals provided transportation, accommodations, and per diem allowances.[12] Customers were told of West Pharmaceuticals' business recovery plans. This was critical because customers needed to know if they will need to find a new supplier of parts. West Pharmaceuticals announced that it would increase production at five other facilities to offset the loss of the Kinston plant. The disruption to the supply chain would be minimal.[13] Customers could prepare for that disruption by adjusting their own production and/or getting additional parts temporarily from another supplier.

The second step is to express concern for the victims. From their first message, West Pharmaceuticals expressed concern for those harmed by the explosion, their friends, and their families. "Our overriding concern lies with the well-being of our employees, their loved ones, and the surrounding community."[14] The concern theme was repeated in later messages. West Pharmaceuticals backed their words with actions. Grief counselors were provided for victims and family members. Employees were told there would be no loss of pay or medical benefits.[15] West Pharmaceuticals also hosted a memorial service to "honor the survivors and commemorate the lives of those that were lost during the Kinston plant tragedy."[16] West Pharmaceuticals spoke of and demonstrated a strong concern for victims.

The final step is to reinforce the accidental nature of the crisis. West Pharmaceutical CEO Don Morel noted, "I think most important here is that when we get to the root cause, it will be an anomaly. I think it will be some unique set of circumstances."[17] Morel described the explosion as something unusual, an accident, something that could not have been anticipated. The implications are that West Pharmaceuticals did not intend for the explosion to occur and probably could not have done anything to prevent this anomaly.

LOSS OF KEY PERSONNEL

The major financial publications spend a lot of time talking about chief executive officers (CEOs) and other top management. The rankings of *Fortune*'s most admired companies is largely a function of the CEO.[18] Who is leading or not leading can have an effect on the organization's stock price and reputation. As a result, the sudden loss of a leader is a threat. The organization needs to reassure stakeholders, mostly stockholders, that it is still in good hands.

Loss of Key Personnel Case: McDonald's CEO

In April 2004, McDonald's CEO Jim Cantalupo was in Orlando, Florida, for McDonald's worldwide owner/operator convention. The event was to be a celebration marking Jim's success in turning McDonald's losses into profits. Under his sixteen-month leadership, McDonald's had seen profits in each of the previous eleven months and an increase in stock price. He was to deliver a presentation and to meet with the participants. He experienced a sudden heart attack in his hotel room and died later in a nearby hospital. He was only sixty years old.

Prevention and Detection

People do die suddenly and unexpectedly. Organizations need to monitor the health of their leadership. The health of the leaders is no longer a private matter but a company matter. Not all leaders are comfortable with that view, but they are important assets and must be monitored. Top leaders can unexpectedly leave a company as well to retire or to accept a better job. If their contracts permit it, leaders can leave as they choose. The best defense against an unexpected departure is a contract that requires a specific amount of notice before an executive leaves.

Basic Crisis Response

The response to loss of key personnel is dual. First, if the loss is a result of illness or a sudden accident, such as a plane crash, the person must be honored and those affected comforted. Consider McDonald's response to Cantalupo's death. The initial statement recognized his achievement and showed concern for those touched by his loss: "Our entire McDonald's system mourns this tragic loss, and our thoughts and prayers are with Jim's wife, Joann, and his family. Our deepest sympathies go out to them. Jim was a brilliant man who brought tremendous leadership, energy and passion to his job. He made an indelible mark on McDonald's system."[19] McDonald's backed words with actions. Full-page advertisements mourning Jim's loss were placed in major newspapers. Flags at McDonald's restaurants were flown at half-mast in his honor.

Second, regardless of the reason for the loss, there must be a smooth transition to the next leader. This is known as a leadership succession plan. The company has a person ready to become the next leader. This is easier to do when you have lead time. However, forward-thinking companies prepare for all eventualities. The day after Cantalupo died, Charlie Bell was elected CEO and Andrew McKenna elected nonexecutive chairman. The announcement stressed how each man had worked closely with Jim and wanted a smooth transition.[20] Although it may seem a little cold to name a replacement so soon, there cannot be a leadership vacuum. Vice presidents are quickly made presidents if the president dies in office. Stakeholders need to be reassured that the company is in good hands. Effective succession provides that valued investor reassurance.

TECHNICAL ERROR TRANSPORTATION MISHAPS

Few crises grab more attention than transportation mishaps. Transportation mishaps are accidents that kill or injure people because a vehicle did not do what it normally does. Planes usually take off and land safely, trains stay on the rails, and buses remain on the road. Accidents are anomalies, and the media are fascinated by oddities. Airline crashes draw the most intense media coverage because of their dramatic nature.[21] Transportation mishaps are limited to those events that were technical errors rather than human error. Technical errors are difficult to detect and often require new procedures to be followed after the fact.

Transportation Mishaps Case: Delta Flight 191

In 1985, Delta experienced a weather-related crash near Dallas, Texas. Flight 191 flew a route from Fort Lauderdale, Florida, to Los

Angeles via Dallas–Fort Worth. On August 2 there were storms in the area. Air traffic control cleared Flight 191 for landing with the warning of a small rain shower in the area. A wind shear—a sudden turbulence that can make it difficult to control an airplane—hit the plane, and it dropped from the skies. A total of 134 passengers and crew were killed, 27 passengers were injured, and miraculously 2 passengers were uninjured. The National Transportation Safety Board (NTSB), the government agency tasked with investigating airline crashes, found one of the primary causes of the accident to be wind shear. Delta argued that the pilots were not properly informed of the risk before attempting the landing.

The airline industry has a history of learning from accidents. Delta Flight 191 raised concern over wind shear. The NTSB had been issuing wind shear concerns for years, but now they became a priority. Wind shear became recognized as a significant hazard in the airline industry. The federal government spent $1.8 million on a training program designed to help pilots identify and handle shifting winds. A congressional hearing paved the way for the installation of Doppler radar to better detect wind shear.[22] The airline industry toughened the detection system for wind shear after the Delta Flight 191 crash. At the time of the crash, wind shear was difficult to detect.

Transportation Mishaps Case: TWA Flight 800

On July 17, 1996, TWA Flight 800 departed New York for Paris. Shortly after takeoff, the Boeing 747 exploded over the Atlantic Ocean. There were no survivors—230 people on board were killed. The incident launched a media and Internet frenzy of activity. This was New York City, a media capital. Then-mayor Rudi Giuliani was not above using the media attention for his own political gain. Many on the Internet talked about Flight 800 being shot down. Some thought the U.S. military had accidentally downed the plane. Others thought terrorists using surface to air missiles had done it. There are still Web sites today that maintain Flight 800 was shot down. For an example of the missile theories, see www.twa800.com.

The NTSB studied the crisis for four years at a cost of $36 million. Their conclusion was that an electrical charge or arcing had caused the center fuel tank to explode. The NTSB recommended that the Federal Aviation Administration (FAA) reevaluate wiring design specifications and recommend improvements. During the course of

the investigation, the NTSB had sent eleven specific recommendations that the FAA acted on. Included in those were inspection of
wiring on Boeing 707s, 737s, 747s, and 767s. A previously unknown technical problem had emerged—wiring near fuel tanks.
TWA Flight 800 was a victim of a technical error, according to the
NTSB.[23]

Prevention and Detection

As with product harm, technical error transportation mishaps are
difficult to prevent and detect. In both of the examples, the situation
might have been averted. Had Doppler radar and other current
detection and prevention practices been in place, Delta Flight 191
might not have crashed. Had someone inspected the wiring on TWA
Flight 800, it might not have exploded. However, at the time, such
detection and prevention was not available. We learn from our
mistakes. Delta Flight 191 did not have advanced wind shear detection technology aiding its approach. Delta's position throughout
was that the crew did not know the danger the plane faced.[24] No one
knew in July 1996 that wiring could be a problem and should be
inspected. Technical error transportation accidents are the warning
signs that serve to prevent additional crises. There are times when a
hidden risk must emerge before it can be recognized.

Basic Crisis Response

Transportation mishaps require notification of next of kin prior to
the release of victims' names. The rule is that every victim's family
must be notified before the list is made public. No partial lists are
given. Giuliani's complaint was that TWA was slow and would not
tell him if a friend was on the flight prior to the public release of the
list. TWA followed the rules. It is difficult to contact family members
on two continents in a short period of time.

Airlines have trauma response units. They go to the scene to aid
victims and family members. The airlines also fly in and care for
family members wanting to visit the crash site. This is all part of
demonstrating concern for victims. Public statements should emphasize the concern for the victims and their families. The public
statement should also note the efforts to help with the investigation.
Once an investigation is completed, an airline should note how it or
the entire industry is implementing the lessons learned from the

tragedy. It should highlight how the lessons will help prevent future accidents.

CHALLENGES

Challenges are a unique crisis. The organization is accused of acting in an immoral or unethical manner. Basically, some group does not like what your company is doing. However, the actions are not illegal, nor do they violate any regulations. The company has to decide if the charges warrant attention and change or should be denied. Sometimes the challenge is a sign that it is time to talk with your stakeholders. The challenge is a concern that could spread to other stakeholders. Management must then decide whether to make a change.

CHALLENGE CASE: WENDY'S AND PETA

People for the Ethical Treat of Animals (PETA) is a group that has launched a number of high-profile challenges against the fast food industry. Their targets are a who's who of fast food: McDonald's, Burger King, Kentucky Fried Chicken, and Wendy's. PETA uses a combination of the Internet and publicity stunts using Hollywood stars to make their challenges public. The idea is that the challenge will pose a reputational and financial threat as it spreads. As a result, the company will be forced into negotiations to change the undesirable behavior. Prior to confronting Wendy's, PETA had successfully changed practices at McDonald's and Burger King, the number one and two fast food giants. Wendy's was next on the list.

In June 2001, PETA told Wendy's that it needed to comply with the animal welfare programs guidelines agreed to by McDonald's and Burger King. Wendy's initial response was that it already did so. PETA then launched the Wicked Wendy campaign to dispute that claim. At the Web site wickedwendy's.com, a menacing Wendy wielded a bloody knife. The site documented Wendy's' noncompliance. To draw media coverage, actor James Cromwell, from the movie *Babe*, and five others were arrested on July 3 for entering a Wendy's in Vienna, Virginia, and telling the lunch crowd not to eat at Wendy's until the company changed how it treated sows.[25] Later that month, PETA and Wendy's began a discussion of the issue.

An agreement was reached in September 2001. PETA ended the Wicked Wendy's campaign by announcing the following:

Wendy's will satisfy PETA's requests that it:
- conduct unannounced inspections of its slaughterhouses and take action against those facilities that fail the inspections.
- institute humane catching guidelines for chickens that will drastically reduce the number of broken bones caused by rough handling.
- require suppliers to give laying hens a minimum of 72 square inches of cage space.
- stop purchasing from suppliers who force-molt (starve chickens in order to force them into laying more eggs).
- immediately require suppliers to adopt air-quality guidelines for chickens.
- improve chicken slaughter methods by increasing the voltage in electric stun baths.
- work to develop alternative housing systems for sows.
- immediately apply the above standards to its Canadian operations.[26]

Challenge Case: Disney Southern Baptist Boycott

On 1997, the Southern Baptist Convention (SBC) voted to boycott Disney. This included Disney's theme parks, products, television, and films. The boycott was implemented because Disney did not meet the SBC's one-year deadline to change its ways. A central complaint was Disney's promotion of a homosexual and antifamily lifestyle. Disney was providing same-sex medical benefits to employees and allowing theme nights in its parks hosted by gay and lesbian groups. Other conservative groups, such as Citizens for a Better America and American Family Association (AFA) joined the SBC. The AFA even produced and distributed a video titled "The Disney Boycott: A Just Cause." (It should be noted that AFA ended its boycott in May 2005, days before starting a boycott of Ford for same-sex benefits, donating to prohomosexual organizations, and using gay themes in some advertising. The boycott was suspended a week later after the AFA met with Ford dealers.)

Unlike Wendy's, Disney was not going to change. Disney spokesperson Ken Green stated the company's basic position: "We are very proud that Disney creates more family entertainment of every kind than anyone else in the world, and we plan to increase that production."[27] Then Disney chief Michael Eisner defended the company in television and print interviews. Disney has kept the same-sex partner benefits and still permits "gay days" at theme parks.

Prevention and Detection

Challenges are generally easy to detect. The unhappy stakeholders often contact an organization before taking action. They move to action when the organization does not respond. PETA first asked McDonald's, Burger King, and Wendy's to make changes. They launched the attacks as way to gain leverage and force the fast food giants to talk about the issues. Similarly, the SBC had complained to Disney prior to the boycott. A smart company will also scan the Internet for any complaints or concerns. (We will talk more about Internet scanning in chapter 5.) Some groups will act before asking the company to change. The crisis might be prevented if management discusses the issue with the concerned stakeholders and resolves it. The company and the unhappy stakeholders need to be able to reach some mutually agreeable solution.

Many different stakeholders can have complaints about improper behavior. You need to make two assessments about a challenge. First, is the concern legitimate? A legitimate concern is one that other stakeholders will agree is valid. An illegitimate concern can be dismissed. Disney did not feel the SBC's concern was legitimate. Initially, Wendy's did not take PETA's concerns seriously.

Second, is the stakeholder group powerful? A stakeholder has power when it can hurt the organization in some way. Boycotts and protests are designed to attract negative media coverage and threaten an organization's reputation. Disney did not feel the SBC had sufficient power to damage their operations or tarnish their reputation. Disney determined this concern was illegitimate and would not harm the company. In fact, most media coverage supported Disney and poked fun at the SBC boycott. In contrast, Wendy's did see PETA as powerful. They were now at the center of negative media coverage and an Internet campaign that had already stung McDonald's and Burger King. Once Wendy's realized PETA's power, the changes in policies were made. A company will likely engage in discussion and make changes during a challenge if the concern is legitimate and the stakeholder has power.

Basic Crisis Response

Challenges present the widest array of responses. An organization can simply deny there is a problem and state why their current actions are appropriate. This was Disney's response to the SBC charges. Only use denial when you have decided the challenge is not worth responding to and/or the stakeholders lack power. On the other extreme is changing to meet the challenge. The company may simply change or negotiate with the stakeholders to reach some mutually agreeable solution. The change option should not be viewed as a signal of weakness. It becomes a strength to listen and to adapt to stakeholders. Organizations can improve performance and relationships by listening to stakeholders and their concerns. Modern public relations practices recommend just such an approach.[28]

SUMMARY: WHAT WE KNOW ABOUT ACCIDENT CRISES

Even the best people and organizations make mistakes. As a result, any organization can have an accident crisis. The unique features of accident crises are the lack of intention and sometimes control. Still accidents turn stakeholders into victims or could harm stakeholders if preventive actions are not taken. This is a threat to an organization as well. Careful monitoring of crisis risks is needed to prevent as many accidents as possible. Crisis managers need to thoughtfully consider what information they need to detect crisis risks and with whom to work to attempt prevention.

When accidents do happen, action must be fast. Crisis managers must send out the instructional information—what stakeholders need to know to protect themselves. The crisis managers also need to express and demonstrate concern for any victims of the crisis. You did not mean for the crisis to happen, but your organization is involved. The legal members of the crisis team can help make sure your sympathy does not become a legal liability. If possible, subtly reinforce the unintended nature of the crisis. You want people talking about the "accident," not the "crisis." The last element of the response is reassurance. Once you know what caused the accident, explain what steps are being taken to prevent a repetition of the events. In the case of lost personnel, emphasize the quality of the new personnel. In each case, the last step is a form a reassurance to stakeholders that the organization has moved past the crisis and is looking toward the future.

4

When the Organization Misbehaves

The worst crisis an organization can face can be one of its own making. Corporate leaders sometimes do bad things that affect the organization and its stakeholders. Enron is the poster child for management misconduct. Stockholders and employees paid a high price for the greed of its leadership. Many other corporate executives have knowingly placed stakeholders at risk or committed serious legal or regulatory violations. Stakeholders are rightfully very upset by management misconduct crises. The stakeholders hold management responsible for the crisis. When officers of the organization are to blame, the reputation damage can be devastating.[1] This chapter will explore the three variations of management misconduct: known risk, improper job performance, and purposeful legal or regulatory violations.

KNOWN RISKS

The desire for profits often leads companies to take shortcuts. These shortcuts can come back to haunt them in the form of a crisis when they create unnecessary risks for stakeholders. A risk is unnecessary when it is known and could have been avoided. Oddly, a central tenet of crisis management is to identify and prevent risk. The need for profit can cause managers to ignore the risk and place stakeholders in danger. The Ford Pinto offers a prime example of known risk that was ignored.

Known Risk Case: Ford Pinto

In the 1960s, Ford was trying to develop a small car to compete with Volkswagen and other imports. The design team was given twenty-five months rather than the typical forty-three to complete the project. Legendary automobile executive Lee Iacocca ran the project. The Pinto project was driven by the number 2,000. The Pinto was to weigh less than 2,000 pounds and cost less than $2,000 (keep in mind, this was the 1960s). Iacocca adhered to the 2,000 figure. He rejected any ideas that would go over 2,000, including ideas to improve the safety of the automobile.

After the production line equipment was set to make cars, the engineers found a flaw. In rear-end collisions, the Pinto's fuel system ruptured easily. The engineers provided two options for fixing the flaw. Both were rejected, and the Pinto went into production with a known flaw. The changes were deemed too costly—finance trumped customer safety. Ford managers actually calculated the costs of making the change verses managing lawsuits from deaths and injuries. The safety change would cost around $11 per car. Based on sales estimates, that would cost Ford a total of $137 million. Accident estimates suggested 2,100 vehicles would burn with 180 serious injuries and 180 deaths. The costs of repairs, injuries, and deaths would total to $49.5 million. The cost-benefit ratio favored the flawed Pinto.

The corrections were actually very simple. In the end, the Ford Pinto cost Ford well over $137 million in lawsuits and unknown costs in the damage to its reputation and relationship with customers. The state of Indiana charged Ford with criminal homicide, the first time such charges were filed against a company. In 1980 Ford was acquitted, and production of the Pinto stopped.[2] The trials documenting the fuel tank problems hurt Pinto sales. Who wants to buy a death trap even if it is cheap? Pinto went from one of Ford's most popular cars to a symbol of corporate greed and callousness.

Trust is the cornerstone of the customer–organization relationship. Conventional wisdom says a company should work hard to keep customers, not run them off because it costs more to attract new customers than to retain old ones. Known risk crises drive off customers. Companies face a steep climb to recover from such crises.

Prevention and Detection

Ford knew there was a risk of fuel tanks exploding in the Pinto. It should be noted that a number of other vehicles by other manufacturers had similar problems in the 1970s. Still, Ford had identified the risk. Their own tests and data from real Pinto accidents all pointed to the fuel tank risk. However, financial factors were granted greater weight, and the risk was accepted. Ford had detected a risk but chose not to take preventive measures. In hindsight, this was a poor choice. The court settlements were far larger than those in the estimates. One case involving a death and one injury cost Ford $6 million (the original award in that case was $125 million, but that was reduced on appeal).[3]

Basic Crisis Response

Ford recalled the Pinto in 1978, but that was too little too late. The recall occurred only after it was recommended by the federal government. Though technically voluntary, the recall was a result of government actions. Ford actively lobbied against laws that would have demanded changes to the Pinto fuel tank for eight years and resisted private calls for a recall. Ford was not responsive to its customers. During a management misconduct crisis, an organization needs to rebuild its reputation by expressing concern for victims and through a series of actions designed to prove it has learned its lesson. This was clearly lacking in Ford's response.

Strangely, the Pinto retains a cult following to this day. There are a number of Ford Pinto clubs, like the Pinto Car Club of America. Scanning the Internet, you can find these groups and their continued devotion to Pintos (such as fordpinto.com). Aside from the fuel tank risk, people loved the little car. But the legacy of the Pinto crisis remains. The fordpinto.com Web site has as one of its goals: "Understand the Ford Motor Company's shortfalls with respect to the Pinto and in no way diminish the importance, the tragedies & the lessons of history & its impact on the present."

IMPROPER JOB PERFORMANCE

It is natural that employees make mistakes on the job. When people do not do what they should, the organization is held responsible, and stakeholders are not very sympathetic. Stakeholders believe that management should ensure that employees do their jobs properly. This means that management properly trains its employees and monitors their performance. As a result, improper job performance is a form of management misconduct crisis. Management is not actively doing anything wrong. Instead, they are guilty of not making sure things are done properly. Improper job performance often has elements of known risk as well. Management might know there is a problem with performance but does nothing to correct or monitor the problem. Air Midwest Flight 5481, the 2005 BP Texas City explosion, and the San Francisco 49ers training tape examples illustrate improper job performance.

Improper Job Performance Case:
Air Midwest Flight 5481

On January 8, 2003, Air Midwest Flight 5481 (d.b.a. US Airways Express) took off from Charlotte-Douglas International Airport in Charlotte, North Carolina. The Beech 1900 was carrying nineteen passengers and two crewmembers. Shortly after takeoff, the plane crashed. There were no survivors. The National Transportation Safety Board (NTSB) identified improper maintenance and improper weight and balance programs by both Air Midwest and the Federal Aviation Administration (FAA) as key contributors to the crash.[4] Raytheon, the company Air Midwest paid to maintain its planes in Huntington, West Virginia, had improperly adjusted the plane's elevator control system. Quality assurance inspectors for the company should have detected the error. The FAA was cited for being lax in monitoring maintenance by Air Midwest, which had a history of improper performance. There was a lack of on-the-job training and supervision of maintenance personnel. Air Midwest's weight and balance program was inaccurate, resulting in improper calculations. The two problems made it difficult for the pilots to control the plan and contributed to the crash.

Prevention and Detection

Air Midwest, Raytheon, and the FAA failed to prevent, detect, and monitor crisis risks. The FAA possessed documentation showing a poor maintenance history for Air Midwest. However, the FAA did not monitor the airline to see if it was correcting the maintenance problems and was meeting federal standards. Air Midwest and Raytheon had flaws in quality assurance. Neither company was making sure the maintenance was done correctly—there was a lack of crisis scanning and monitoring. Improper maintenance is a common risk in airlines. Air Midwest should have been trying to detect new risks and monitoring old ones to see that the risks had been addressed. Air Midwest knew it had a problem with maintenance but did little to correct the risk. A known risk was allowed to flourish and resulted in the loss of twenty-one lives. There was lack of prevention and detection.

Basic Crisis Response

Christiana Shepard, the eighteen-year-old daughter of Pastor Douglas and Tereasa Shepherd, was among those who died on Flight 5481. The Shepards wanted more than a monetary settlement from Air Midwest. As part of their settlement terms, the family demanded a public apology from Air Midwest to settle a wrongful death claim stemming from the crash. They wanted those responsible for the crash to hold themselves accountable and publicly apologize to the victims' families. On May 6, 2005, Greg Stephens, president of Air Midwest, read the following statements to the families of seven victims gathered in Charlotte:

> We are here today to remember the victims of Flight 5481 and to offer our apologies, condolences and sincere sympathy to the surviving family members of the passengers and crew who perished in the January 8, 2003 crash of Air Midwest Flight Number 5481. We are deeply saddened by your loss. The National Transportation Safety Board's investigation disclosed

errors that caused and contributed to this tragic accident. We participated fully with the NTSB in its investigation and understand our roles leading up to the crash. Air Midwest and its maintenance provider, Vertex, acknowledge deficiencies, which together with the wording of the aircraft maintenance manuals, contributed to this accident. This tragedy has caused us to investigate rigorously our policies and guidelines regarding aircraft maintenance, operation and safety in general. We have taken substantial measures to prevent similar accidents and incidents in the future, so that your losses will not have been suffered in vain. We have also implemented or are implementing the applicable NTSB safety recommendations following this accident. We are truly sorry, and regret and apologize to everyone affected by this tragic event.[5]

Two years after the crash, Air Midwest had delivered the proper crisis response under legal pressure. Management took responsibility for the misconduct crisis, expressed sympathy for those involved, and outlined corrective actions to prevent a repeat of the crisis. The response would have had a greater positive effect had it been delivered earlier and was not part of a legal settlement. Even so, the Air Midwest apology provides an effective illustration of how a company should respond when it knows it is to blame.

Improper Job Performance Case: BP Texas City

On March 23, 2005, a deadly blast ripped through the BP Products North America facility at Texas City, Texas. The event happened during the start-up of the isomerization unit. The blast killed 17 and injured over 170 people. Within months, BP and government officials agreed that the accident should never have happened. BP officials had not installed a more effective flare safety system that could have prevented the blast. Moreover, BP management had not followed safety procedures during the start-up. Management did not ensure that the proper procedures were being followed, and trailers used for temporary offices were located in an area that was in danger, but no warning was issued. Many of the injured were personnel near the trailers who should have been told to evacuate when the problem first developed.[6] The initial government investigation also noted a failure to use the warning system. In addition, government officials had told BP thirteen years before that the facility should switch its blow-down stack system with a more effective flare system.[7] The bottom line: The BP tragedy was preventable. Actions not taken by BP management placed stakeholders at risk with deadly consequences.

Prevention and Detection

Texas City offers a perfect example of the need for detection and prevention. During the start-up, critical alarms and equipment that would have warned operators of a problem were not in use. As a result, operators did not know they were overloading the system and creating a possible explosion.[8] Detection on the day of the accident might have prevented the tragedy. BP and government regulators had detected the risk of relying on the blow-down stack system. BP management failed to reduce the risk from the isomerization unit by not installing a flare system. The March 23 blast proved the government's point that the blow-down stack was not a very effective safety system. BP management should have changed to a flare system to reduce the risk and prevent just such a tragedy. BP could have used prevention to avoid this event.

BP management also failed to monitor safety compliance. Management personnel were not using proper safety procedures. The safety procedures were known. Many organizations monitor compliance with safety procedures as a mean of making sure workers follow those procedures. If management fails to show a concern for safety, safety procedures are ignored and the risk for a serious incident increases. In addition to reviewing accident data, crisis managers should work with other units to ensure safety reviews occur and the value of safety procedures is reinforced.

Basic Crisis Response

BP has accepted responsibility for the accident. Here is part of their statement:

> "The mistakes made during the startup of this unit were surprising and deeply disturbing. The result was an extraordinary tragedy we didn't foresee," said Ross Pillari, president of BP Products North America, Inc.
> "We regret that our mistakes have caused so much suffering. We apologize to those who were harmed and to the Texas

City community. We cannot change the past or repair all the damage this incident has done. We can assure that those who were injured and the families of those who died receive financial support and compensation. Our goal is to provide fair compensation without the need for lawsuits or lengthy court procedures."[9]

BP backed its words with action—management moved swiftly to settle wrongful death lawsuits. No final figure has been given, but the settlement is in the millions of dollars per family. BP chose to work with the lawyers of the victims' families rather than fight them in court. Their words and actions reflect an acceptance of responsibility and concern for the victims. This is exactly the type of response that is needed if an organization is to begin repairing the damage that management misconduct crisis rains down on an organization. BP took a much more accommodating approach to the crisis than did Ford in the Pinto crisis. Both companies were responsible for placing stakeholders at risk but enacted very different strategies to respond to the crisis. BP also responded much faster than did Air Midwest.

Improper Job Performance Case:
49ers Training Video

This last case study is one of the oddest forms of management misconduct. The best way to describe it is stupidity. In spring 2005, the *San Francisco Chronicle* exposed a disturbing in-house training video produced by public relations director Kirk Reynolds of the NFL football team the San Francisco 49ers. The training video was designed to teach players how to handle the news media in a diverse community and was shown to players during the August 2004 training camp. The video contained a variety of racial slurs and what some called lesbian pornography. A newspaper article detailed the events depicted in the video, and readers could view the video at the newspaper's Web site. The video cast the 49ers organization in a very unfavorable light, drawing condemnations from the gay community, Asian community, and the mayor of San Francisco.[10]

Kirk Reynolds lost his job, and the top management of the team apologized for the offensive video that was said by the team's lawyer to be "absolutely contradictory to the ideals and values of the San

Francisco 49ers."[11] The average person would not consider the material appropriate for company training. In this case, at least one manager did (Reynolds), and the organization was placed at risk by his choices. Reynolds and others should have known there would be risk of negative reactions if the video were ever made public.

Prevention and Detection

Not everyone in the 49ers organization thought the video was a good idea. The former general manager showed the owner clips of the video in January 2005. As previous cases have shown, misconduct becomes a crisis when management detects a risk but does nothing about it. The team owner, who offered up a public apology and condemned the action in June, did nothing about the video and risk in January. The team management lost credibility as it addressed a known problem only after the news media revealed it.

Basic Crisis Response

In June 2005, the 49ers' management was quick to respond. The owners made the following statement:

> The San Francisco 49ers apologize for the inappropriate and tasteless video produced as part of a player training program this past season. Ostensibly, the video was created to raise player awareness about how to deal with the media and to demonstrate by example how poor conduct can unintentionally make news. Unfortunately, this video is an example in itself.
>
> The video is offensive in every manner. We deeply regret that anyone from our organization would produce such senseless, inexcusable material. A thorough investigation of this issue has been ongoing for some time, and actions and disciplines have been taken. Policies are being put into place to ensure that nothing like this ever happens again. The individuals responsible for producing the video have left or are leaving our employment.
>
> The content of this training material was never cleared by any officer of this organization and is absolutely contradictory to the ideals and values of the San Francisco 49ers. The 49ers

have zero tolerance for anything that ridicules this city or any segment of the population, or for anything that creates an environment that anyone could find harassing, embarrassing or uncomfortable.

Our team is proud to represent San Francisco and the Bay Area. This incident is not reflective of our franchise, our organization, our team or the millions of fans that support the 49ers.

We promote diversity and understanding of all lifestyles and viewpoints, but there is clearly a need for more emphasis or a different approach. We plan to expand our efforts to ensure that every member of our team—athletes and front office personnel—understands the importance of this perspective.

Sincerely,

Denise and John York[12]

The response featured the requirements for an effective mismanagement response. The action was deemed wrong, an apology offered, responsibility accepted, corrective actions taken, and sympathy and regret expressed. The only problem was that John York knew of the videotape in January. Prior knowledge lessened the impact of the statement. Reporters questioned why action was taken then and not in January if York truly believed the tape was inappropriate. Doubts will plague management misconduct responses when stakeholders feel the organization should have taken action sooner. Still, the adage "better late than never" applies to this case. The organization is learning, albeit slowly.

PURPOSEFUL LEGAL/REGULATORY VIOLATIONS

There are times when management knowingly engages in illegal activities. Enron is the prime example. Top executives hid debt from the financial community to inflate stock prices and make money. This can be called corporate corruption. People in management use their positions of trust and power to benefit themselves, often at the expense of others. The defining characteristic is that the managers know they are violating some law or regulation. The widespread sexual harassment at Mitsubishi and the looting of Tyco will illustrate the purposeful legal/regulatory violations.

Purposeful Legal/Regulatory Violation Case: Mitsubishi Sexual Harassment

You would think nothing odd ever happens in a town called Normal. In 1996, the Equal Employment Opportunity Commission (EEOC) filed a major sexual harassment lawsuit against automobile manufacturer Mitsubishi. The suit claimed that over 300 female employees had been harassed at the facility through a variety of lewd behaviors that included obscene gestures, groping, and the display of pornographic pictures. The EEOC stated, "The already available evidence indicates that the magnitude and scope of sexual and sex-based harassment at Mitsubishi, and the degree of managerial complicity therein, are unprecedented."[13] Before the final settlement in June 1998, Mitsubishi was being boycotted by Jesse Jackson's Rainbow Coalition and the National Organization for Women. Mitsubishi hired former Secretary of Labor Lynn Martin to investigate the situation. Her report condemned Mitsubishi management for allowing the harassing behavior to continue. Management had known of the problems and risk but done little to protect the stakeholders (employees).[14]

Prevention and Detection

Martin's report indicated that management at Mitsubishi had successfully detected the problem years before and knew that sexual harassment was occurring. However, management did very little to address the risk. Instead, the problem festered and worsened. Management knowingly allowed a risk to thrive. Had action been taken earlier to eradicate the sexual harassment problem, Mitsubishi would never have become one of the worst cases in U.S. history. The company would have saved itself the public embarrassment and expenses created by the crisis. Once more, we learn that detection means little if there are no efforts to prevent.

Basic Crisis Response

Mitsubishi's initial response was a textbook case of the "circle the wagons" response. Management denied any wrongdoing and claimed that the EEOC was harassing them. Mitsubishi even paid to have 2,700 workers bused three hours to Chicago to protest at the EEOC offices there. Mitsubishi paid for the buses, lunch, and even the wages of the workers who went. A few months later the company shifted the response. Martin was hired to investigate. A new department was formed to investigate sexual harassment claims, and all workers went through eight hours of sexual harassment training.[15] Finally, management did admit the problem once they had the report from Martin. Over a two-year period, Mitsubishi settled private lawsuits against it and finally the EEOC case, for which the company paid $34 million to 350 female employees. The response was slow but eventually did compensate stakeholders, take corrective action, and accept some responsibility. As with Air Midwest, the response would have been more impressive and effective had it happened much earlier in the crisis.

Purposeful Legal/Regulatory Violation Case: Tyco's Legal Violations

The year 2002 was a dark year for Tyco International, once the darling of Wall Street. In 2002, CEO Dennis Kozlowski and a number of other top management resigned under pressure. Soon Tyco revealed that through improper use of power, these people had illegally taken over $600 million from the company. Their tactics involved the misuse of a variety of Tyco compensation programs, such as relocation, bonuses, automotive bonuses, and a employee loan program. Kozlowski was the central spider spinning a web of deceit. He hid transactions from the board of directors' compensation committee while telling lower ranking managers that the actions were board-approved. Kozlowski's most publicized misappropriation was a $1 million party for his wife. The bill was charged to Tyco for an extravagant party in Sardinia that featured an ice sculpture of David that urinated high-priced vodka. On June 17, 2005, Kozlowski and others were convicted in state court for misappropriation of funds and subsequently sentenced to jail time in September 2005.

The damage to Tyco was significant. The stock price plummeted as investors lost confidence in the once-mighty company. In the words of a Tyco news release: "Kozlowski breached these duties to the Company and, as a result, the Company has been damaged in an amount that far exceeds the amounts that Kozlowski directly misappropriated for himself. To hold him accountable for his misconduct, we seek not only full payment for the funds he misappropriated but also punitive damages for the serious harm he did to Tyco and its shareholders."[16] The financial losses were compounded with reputational loss. Investors, a key stakeholder group, had lost trust in Tyco.

Prevention and Detection

Tyco illustrated the dangers of corrupt top management acting secretly to drain financial resources from a firm. WorldCom and Adelphia are two other companies that suffered similar fates. It is difficult to detect management corruption. Detection requires close examination of accounting methods by auditors who are independent of the company—not beholden to the people they are reviewing. Enron taught a valuable lesson of what happens when auditors do not really try to detect problems. Prevention requires managers and corporate boards who will act when the problems are revealed. Kozlowski did an excellent job of hiding his activities. Still, a more suspicious system would have looked more closely at his actions rather than letting him run amuck. Experts refer to this as governance failure. The board of directors did not properly oversee the activities of the CEO. Companies need accounting systems that will review all members of management and board members who take this responsibility seriously and hold management accountable for their actions. The Sarbanes-Oxley legislation of 2002 was the government's attempt to reinforce the importance of financial oversight. Sarbox, as it is known, should make it easier to detect financial games by top managers.

Basic Crisis Response

Tyco needed to rebound from the corruption charges. The first action was to purge Tyco of all those involved in Kozlowski's web. Those involved resigned or were fired in 2002. Tyco then filed charges against those involved and detailed their exact misappropriations in news releases. A new CEO, Edward Breen, was hired to help rebuild confidence. He would create a new management team and management structure that would restore Tyco's reputation by rebuilding trust with stakeholders. In his initial letter to employees, Breen stated:

> Now that I'm with Tyco and the leadership transition is moving forward, I am determined to focus on these immediate priorities:

- First, we must have an absolute commitment to integrity and trustworthiness throughout the organization. That is a fundamental imperative.
- With that commitment, we will establish Tyco as a leader in creating and enforcing the best corporate governance practices.
- We will continue our relentless dedication to customer satisfaction, with consistently superior products and service.
- We will continue to build our operating businesses—the heart of this company—and strengthen the leadership positions they hold in their industries.
- The growth of the operating businesses will create new opportunities and the most positive work environment possible for the employees of Tyco.
- If we do all this well, as I commit to you we shall, we will restore Tyco's credibility with all our constituencies and build value for our shareholders.[17]

Obviously the key was corporate governance. Failed governance was what allowed Kozlowski to loot Tyco, so that needed fixing. Breen emphasized the governance concern in his letter.

With regard to one of the key priorities I have mentioned, corporate governance, I am pleased to tell you that we have retained a widely recognized and respected expert on these matters, Michael Useem. He is Director of the Wharton Center for Leadership and Change Management and Professor of Management in the Wharton School at the University of Pennsylvania. Professor Useem has worked with many companies on successful programs of leadership change and governance and has written extensively on these topics. I have given Michael the following responsibilities: (1) develop an objective, thorough and specific analysis of what constitutes the best corporate governance practices; (2) assess, objectively and in depth, this company's practices, compared to the best corporate practices; (3) make specific recommendations as to how to implement and enforce the best practices at Tyco; and (4) work with me and the Board to ensure that necessary changes are made quickly and effectively. Michael is to begin his work immediately.[18]

Eric Pillman was hired by Tyco as internal governance watchdog with the title of senior vice president of corporate governance. He created and then enforced the new employee ethical code of conduct at Tyco. Pillman was one example of how CEO Breen was bringing in new people with a record of good work and an ability to fix problems. Tyco lost $9 billion in 2002 but by 2004 had generated a profit of $40 billion. Tyco stock prices rebounded as well. Stock analysts and investors had new confidence that Tyco has fixed its management problems and still had the core assets that made it such a profitable company in the past.[19] To some, the quick comeback was a miracle. On closer inspection, the comeback was the result of effective strategic action by Breen and others on the new management team.

SUMMARY: WHAT WE KNOW FROM THE MANAGEMENT MISCONDUCT CASES

Management misconduct crises come in three varieties: known risk, improper job performance, and purposeful legal or regulatory violation. The shared trait is that stakeholders believe all of these crises should be prevented. Management should take steps to address a known risk, should strive for proper job performance, and obey laws and regulations. We can debate which is the worst type of management misconduct, but all are harmful or deadly.

Prevention and Detection

Organizations need to monitor all of the systems that can generate crisis risk. Most have mechanisms for monitoring safety and accounting. However, this monitoring is not always serious. People are not trying to detect and prevent risks; they are often only shuffling paper. Crisis managers need to have the mechanisms in place to detect and to prevent risks. Crisis risks must be highlighted and taken seriously within the organization. Having an established crisis management system at the highest levels of management will reinforce the value of tackling crisis risks. A system for detection must be in place along with a commitment to prevention. If all crises have warning signs or prodromes, the challenge is to find those signs. With management misconduct crises, the signs should be easy to find if the organization is committed to doing that. Having an independent crisis manager searching for symptoms increases the chance of discovering acts of management misconduct.

Basic Crisis Response

Management misconduct crises are the most challenging to handle. The crisis erodes trust, the centerpiece of the organization–stakeholder relationship. These crises pose the greatest reputational and financial risk to an organization. The cases provide a number of lessons.

1. Express concern/sympathy for victims immediately. The focus on the response needs to be on the victims from the very start. Stakeholders expect management to acknowledge the victims. Concern or sympathy can be expressed without incurring financial liability for the crisis.
2. If the organization is clearly at fault, accept responsibility and apologize early, at the start. Put more simply, if you know you are wrong, admit it. Accepting responsibility means the organization will have to pay the victims. Better to settle early than to drag it out in court. Extended court cases only prolong the negative publicity and increase the amount the victims will want. BP admitted responsibility and began settling claims quickly. There are times when an investigation is needed before responsibility can be determined. As a result, the apology and responsibility acceptance may come later, as was the case with Air Midwest.
3. Explain what the organization has done to prevent a repeat of the crisis. This is known as corrective action. To rebuild trust, stakeholders need to know the organization has learned its lesson and is unlikely to repeat the violation in the future. Corrective action requires an investigation that locates the cause(s) of the crisis. Tyco and Mitsubishi both engaged in extensive corrective action.
4. Think how stakeholders will react if the actions are reported in the news media. How will they feel about the decision? Do you believe you can publicly defend your actions? Any managers

who are thinking about exposing stakeholders to a known risk should consider such questions. Can you convince stakeholders that it was okay to place them at risk? If you answer "no," rethink your options.

II

CRISIS MANAGEMENT

5

Crisis-Sensing Network

The problems with Firestone tires and Ford Explorers became a worldwide crisis in 2000. In the end, over 6.5 million tires were recalled and two longtime business partners became bitter enemies. Firestone and Ford had been connected through decades of business and even marriages among the families. (The current Fords are also Firestones.) Each company blamed the other for the tire blowouts and deaths. As a result, Ford replaced Firestone as a tire supplier. Crisis expert Stephen Fink claims that every crisis has a warning sign. He calls these warning signs *prodromes*.[1] A State Farm Mutual Automobile Insurance employee was the first to see the prodromes for the Firestone-Ford crisis. As early as 1997, State Farm had noticed an unusually high number of accidents involving Firestone tires. The initial concerns were relayed to the National Highway Traffic Safety Administration (NHTSA) in 1998.[2]

In 1998, State Farm employee Sam Boyden began looking at the Firestone-related accidents more closely. His research documented the link between the Firestone tires and Ford Explorer. The NHTSA did not respond to his first report. Boyden continued studying the accidents in 1999 and found the same pattern. Again a message was sent to the NHTSA. This time the agency responded and began its own investigation. Boyden was the only person to see the pro-drome. Employees at Ford and Firestone had access to the same data, but the evidence went unnoticed there.[3]

Not all prodromes are easy to see. However, some seem to be invisible even when they should be obvious. Remember how management misconduct crises can emerge even when the warning signs were clear. Sometimes people try to hide the prodromes. However, the main problem is a failure to scan for risks and crisis. Organizations need to continually look for potential crises. I refer to this as a crisis-sensing network. When crisis management is part of the company's DNA, there will be a crisis-sensing network devoted to detecting and preventing crisis risks. Companies that simply add-on crisis management will not have this same level of commitment, nor will they develop the mechanisms necessary for crisis sensing. This chapter outlines what crisis sensing is, how to create an effective crisis-sensing system, and the value of the Internet and intranets to crisis sensing.

WHAT IS A CRISIS-SENSING NETWORK?

It is a fact that preparation is the key to effective crisis management. Another fact is that it is better to prevent a crisis than to experience a crisis. Prevention can save lives, money, and reputations.[4] A few experts argue that certain crises are necessary to create change. However, a crisis is a poor method of change management. Detection is the key to prevention. To prevent a potential crisis you must first identify it. Crisis managers must search for prodromes, symptoms, or warning signs. Warning signs are weaknesses or risks that could develop into a crisis. For instance, a series of small chemical spills is a warning that a larger spill could occur. The small spills suggest that there is something wrong with how chemicals are being handled. Actions should be taken to identify and correct the problem(s). Detection should feed into prevention.

Hail and cars do not mix very well. A fear at any automobile assembly plant is that the acres of vehicles waiting to be shipped might be hit and damaged by hail. When Nissan built its facility near Canton, Mississippi, the company became proactive with hail. Their vehicle storage area excedes 140 acres. A hail storm would result in millions of dollars of damage. Nissan purchased and installed an antihail system. The system is based on detection and prevention. The machine has its own weather equipment that can detect when conditions are right for hail to form. When hail conditions are detected, the machine fires sonic waves up to 50,000 feet in the air every 5.5 seconds. The sonic waves are designed to prevent the development of hail. The sounds are about as loud as a tornado siren.[5] Although unpleasant, a little noise is better than millions of dollars in hail damage. The crisis-sensing network works much the same way for crises. The network finds the crisis risk *before* the crisis hits, and actions are taken to prevent its development.

Prodromes rarely announce themselves to people in the organization; you need to actively search for them. A crisis-sensing network is systematic means of collecting prodrome-related information. Think of the crisis-sensing network as prodrome radar. The basic idea is that any information about crisis risks (possible prodromes) is delivered to a crisis manager for review. The network becomes the eyes and ears of the crisis manager. An individual or team systematically sifts through the information for prodromes. The term *systematic* is important. Most organizations collect information that might contain prodromes. However, not all of them systematically examine the information to locate prodromes. For years, Ford and Firestone did not see the tire crisis. Another example: The September 11, 2001, report noted that the FBI needed more analysts to examine the intelligence data it was collecting at the time.

The *Titanic* provides an excellent example of how not being systematic can allow a crisis to unfold. Through movies, television, and books, most people are familiar with the sinking of the *Titanic*. Historians often describe the *Titanic* crisis as "if only." There are a long list of actions that if only they had been taken, the megaliner may not have crashed or the loss of life might not have been so great. The short list includes: lookouts for icebergs not having binoculars that night, canceled lifeboat drills for passengers, crew underloading lifeboats because they did not know their true capacity, and failure to integrate warnings.

For crisis sensing, the failure to integrate information is a focal point. In the most recent movie of the *Titanic* tragedy, the captain places a warning about icebergs in his pocket without reading it. Nice dramatic touch, but the reality was even worse. The *Titanic* had received numerous warnings of ice before the crash. These warnings were being sent by other ships that had seen the ice. The warnings indicated where the *Titanic* might encounter icebergs. Some warnings were never given to the captain. The warnings were never integrated; they were simply individual statements. Had the *Titanic* crew plotted each warning, they would have realized the ship was in the middle of a fairly large ice field. Logic would then dictate traveling at a lower speed. The *Titanic* had been traveling at full speed to make sure it arrived as scheduled. At a slower speed, the ship might not have hit the iceberg or might have sustained less damage and remained afloat. The failure to systematically review the prodrome-related information may have doomed thousands of people.[6]

Of course the *Titanic* example also reveals the power of hindsight. It is easy for us to see the problems now. This is true of most crises. The skill is finding and understanding a prodrome in real time. However, you will never find them if you do not have a system for locating the necessary information. The post–September 11 environment in the United States has pushed the federal government in the direction of crisis sensing. The National Research Council has proposed a nationwide system for collecting and managing bioterrorism-related information.[7] The revision of the U.S. intelligence agencies is an example of trying to get information to the right people. A crisis-sensing network does just that. It identifies and delivers potential crisis-related information to crisis managers.

A crisis-sensing network has two critical features: information collection and analysis. Sensing starts with scanning for information. Scanning includes any efforts to collect information, including requests for information.[8] But collecting information is not enough. As managers now realize, there is a difference between information and knowledge. Information becomes knowledge when someone examines and evaluates the information.[9] If you collect crisis-related information but never examine it, you will not locate prodromes.

The deadly December 2004 tsunami illustrates collection and analysis. After a massive earthquake, a number of scientists realized there could be a tsunami. No one knew how big, but they knew one was likely. The U.S. National Oceanic and Atmospheric Administration had the information but did not know to whom they should send it. The countries involved had not taken steps to collect this type of crisis information. Another scientist tried calling the proper official in Thailand but could not get through due to a busy signal.[10] Again, the system for collecting information was weak.

Tsunamis have a pattern, which is noticeable if someone understands that pattern. Before the major wave strikes, the tide goes out suddenly and far. In the 2004 tsunami, many unfortunate individuals went down to the beach to see this event. Few understood the information and were able to convert it into usable knowledge of a tsunami. One exception was ten-year old Tilly Smith. Tilly was from the United Kingdom and was in Phuket, Thailand, enjoying a vacation with her parents. When Tilly saw the tide so far out at Maikao beach, she knew a wave might follow. Tilly had recently completed a school report about tsunamis. Her mother alerted the hotel staff, and the beach was evacuated. Maikao was one of the few beaches in Thailand where no one was killed. Tilly collected and analyzed the information about the tsunami prodrome.[11] Unfortunately, many others did not understand what they were seeing. The discussion of how to create a crisis-sensing network reflects the need for both collection and analysis of information.

CREATING A CRISIS-SENSING NETWORK

Most organizations will find they already have a strong base for creating a crisis-sensing network. The raw materials will be there. People need to organize and refine these materials into a finished product. The crisis-sensing network becomes a part of how the organization operates—crisis management as DNA. The most efficient way to construct a crisis-sensing network is to answer a series of questions. There is no single perfect crisis-sensing mechanism for every organization. The unique aspects of each organization demand that the network be crafted to its needs. These questions are designed to highlight the information that will allow an organization to create its own crisis-sensing network.

1. What Crisis Risks Does the Organization Face?

A common starting point for crisis management is to generate a list of all the possible crises that could hit your organization. This activity is known as the crisis risk assessment. Different organizations face different types of crises. A casino and a chemical manufacturer do not face the same list of potential crises. A casino will have concerns related to guests, such as evacuating during a fire or the possibility of food poisoning. Chemical manufacturers have concerns over exposure to hazardous materials and explosions. In reality, you are creating a list of crisis risks rather than a list of actual crises. You understand the risks you face by confronting the crises you might have. Sources of risk include personnel, the production process itself, materials and equipment used in the production process, goods or services created, and geographic location. Table 5.1 provides a more detailed list of crisis risks.

TABLE 5.1: POSSIBLE CRISIS RISKS
Customers
Complaints
Misuse of product
Challenges
Product harm
Suppliers
Disruption from crises
Suddenly go out of business
Location
Natural disasters
Near potential terrorist targets (e.g., transportation center, financial district, etc.)
Transportation disruption (employees cannot get to work)
Affected by crisis at nearby organizations (e.g., chemical release)
Employees
Accidents
Sabotage
Workplace violence
Illness
Production Process
Chemicals and other materials used in the process
Process itself
Equipment used in process
Software used in the process
Management
Violation of laws or regulations
Abuse of power
Illness or death
Computer Systems
External attacks
Power failures
Loss of data

A comprehensive list of the risks that could become a crisis for your organization provides the best starting point.[12]

2. How Can You Scan for Each Crisis Risk?

Crisis risks are the sources of prodromes. A crisis risk is a potential source of a crisis. Changes in the crisis risk indicate the potential development of a crisis. For instance, employees not following safety procedures will open the doors for a crisis. Accidents are more likely when safety is ignored. Lack of safety oversight and/or minor accidents become prodromes. Review your list of crisis risks. Identify at least one mechanism for scanning each and every crisis risk. There is no need to reinvent the wheel. Audit your current organizational sensing activities. Organizations typically monitor a number of areas related to crisis risk. A typical list includes customer complaints, accident records, regulatory audits, and insurance reviews. Compare your list of crisis risks that need to be scanned with those you currently scan. Add new sources if your current practices do not cover your entire list.

3. Is Crisis Risk Information Delivered to the Crisis Manager?

The crisis-sensing mechanism should funnel all risk-relevant information to the crisis manager/crisis management unit. A crisis manager or unit cannot find prodromes if the relevant information does not reach them. A variety of organizational units will be involved in collecting crisis information, including operations and manufacturing, marketing and sales, finance, human resources, customer relations, security, and quality assurance. Other organizational units must understand that it is important to forward the required information to the crisis management unit. The crisis manager is the epicenter of the crisis-sensing mechanism. The crisis manager/unit must be treated as a functioning unit that is integrated within the flow of organizational information not a team that is called solely when a crisis hits.

By having information from a wide array of units, crisis managers have the potential to perceive a risk from multiple perspectives. The perspectives should make it easier to identify the prodrome before it develops into a crisis. An example would be reports from quality assurance and customer relations that suggest a product defect may be placing customers at risk.

4. How Is the Crisis Risk Information Being Processed into Crisis Knowledge?

This question assumes that crisis risk information is being processed, not simply dumped into the crisis management unit. The problem with an elaborate crisis-sensing mechanism is that it will collect a large amount of information. However, if the information is not processed into knowledge—if someone does not evaluate the information—the network is pointless. As with the *Titanic*, the prodrome is never identified because no one has put the pieces of the crisis risk together.

Each organization needs to develop criteria for evaluating risks. The system will be built around the two fundamental criteria in crisis management: likelihood and impact. *Likelihood* is the probability that a risk will develop into a crisis. You are trying to determine how likely it is that the risk will become an actual crisis. We have a greater awareness of tsunamis in the United States following the devastation in Asia. However, the likelihood of a tsunami hitting California is unlikely. *Impact* is the effect a crisis will have on an organization if it does occur. You are trying to assess how badly the crisis would affect the organization if it did occur. An airliner crash has a huge impact on the organization, while an airplane sliding off a runway has a smaller impact.

Crisis managers need to decide how they will evaluate likelihood and impact—what specific criteria they will apply to the risks they identify. Crisis managers must understand why one risk is given a 3 and another is given a 6. This means that people understand and can apply the criteria used to evaluate crisis risks. The crisis unit needs to develop specific criteria and be sure everyone in the unit knows how to apply the criteria. Generally each risk is given a score of 1 to 10 with 10 representing the highest risk. One formula for risk is likelihood (L) multiplied by impact (I) equals crisis risk (CR). The higher the crisis risk, the more attention the crisis management unit needs to place on that risk.[13] Table 5.2 illustrates some hypothetical crisis risk assessments.

TABLE 5.2:
SAMPLE CRISIS RISK ASSESSMENT

Organization: Resort Hotel Located near the coast of North Carolina

A. Hotel Fire

Likelihood is moderate	4
Impact is high but safety precaution and technology help reduce it	8

4 (L) × 8 (I) = 32 (CR)

B. Category Four Hurricane

Likelihood is very low	2
Impact is very high because of threat to people and property	10

2 (L) × 10 (I) = 20 (CR)

Even though a fire will have less of an impact, the greater likelihood makes it a greater threat. There are many possible sources of a fire that are difficult to control, especially actions by guests such as smoking and leaving irons on unattended. A hurricane has but one source. Moreover, the government should give you ample warning about a hurricane and history suggests such a strong hurricane is unlikely to hit your area.

---

5. Has the Crisis-Sensing Network Been Tested?

As with a crisis management plan, merely having a crisis-sensing network does not mean it is effective. The system must be tested. You can test the flow and processing of crisis risk information by simply placing selected information into the various branches on the system and monitor how it moves through the network. The crisis-sensing network is evaluated by determining if the information reaches the crisis managers, how long it takes the information to reach crisis managers, how long it takes the crisis managers to evaluate the information, and how accurate the evaluation of the information was. You need to evaluate both collection and analysis. The crisis-sensing network is a complex communication/information processing system that requires regular checking and refinement to maintain and improve its efficiency. As with any skill in an organization, crisis sensing improves with practice and experience.[14] Crisis managers needed to be trained and tested in their crisis-sensing skills and ability to operate the crisis-sensing network.

TECHNOLOGICAL AIDS

Technology can aid in crisis sensing. The aids come in three forms: (1) identifying risks, (2) channeling information, and (3) analyzing risks.

The Internet

The Internet offers a wealth of valuable information mixed with some of the worst information. Still, it is an excellent tool for locating some crisis risks. Customers may provide information about potential problems when they post messages at discussion groups, complaint portals, or to their own blogs. The first challenge is to find these messages. Search engines help. You can regularly search your organization's name and the names of its key products or services. You can also visit relevant discussion groups and complaint portals for information. If you have the money you can hire a firm such as CyberAlert or eWatch to do the searching for you. Such companies can provide you with summaries as well as copies of the references to your organization that they have found. The Internet should be one of the tools in your crisis-sensing network.

An Intranet

Intranets are secure sites only people in your organization can access. This is an excellent way to share crisis risk information. Other units can forward the information to the crisis unit. The crisis unit can then organize the information. The best way would be to create folders for each of the crisis risks your organization has identified. Incoming information is then placed in one or more folders according to the risk. Multiple folders may be needed because some information may apply to more than one crisis risk. An intranet also supplies a quick means of requesting additional information. If the crisis management unit needs to ask a follow-up question, the intranet can be used to document the request and the response.

Analytic Aids

There are a variety of software packages that use a form of content analysis to aid analysis. Content analysis here means that the software looks for key words in documents you have collected. For instance, some e-mail filters block messages that contain certain unacceptable words and report the e-mail to administrators. This is how companies learn when an employee is sending improper messages. Similarly, the software can be instructed to look for key words that relate to a crisis risk such as "defect," "accident," or "incident." Then each key word will be fitted to the crisis risk. Your crisis-sensing mechanism will generate a great deal of information, and analyzing all of it may take too much time. The idea is that the software can help find the most relevant pieces of information for further analysis.

Although it is clearly a benefit, technology has its limits. Technology does not replace the need for people. Do not think that an automated crisis-sensing network is a great idea. Technology can aid analysis, but it never replaces human analysis. Consider that your computer's spell checker still misses over 10 percent of your errors. Much more time, research, and testing has gone into your spell checker than the technologies that aid crisis sensing. Human eyes are still needed.

SUMMARY

A crisis-sensing network is critical if an organization wants to make crisis management part of its DNA. The crisis-sensing network reinforces the idea that crisis management is an everyday activity and that the crisis management unit is an integral part of the organization. A crisis-sensing network takes a greater commitment than simply having a plan. The organization must commit to having a crisis manager or management unit that receives and evaluates crisis risk-related information. This requires staffing and developing structures that facilitate the flow of information to the crisis management unit. Chapter 7 will discuss how to build support for such efforts.

An effective crisis-sensing network will help spot and prevent many crises. Will it catch all potential crises? No. No system is perfect. Some crisis risks that are rated low may quickly morph into a crisis. Although all crises have prodromes, this does not mean a crisis manager will see or recognize every one. However, the odds of preventing a crisis increase greatly when an organization has an effective crisis-sensing network.

6

The Crisis Management Plan as Living Document

From the start of this book I have argued that a crisis management plan is not sufficient for managing a crisis. But there is no denying that a crisis management plan (CMP) is a vital part of any crisis management effort. The CMP should be treated as a starting point rather than an end point. With the CMP comes the need for training. People need to practice using the plan. The value of various training methods will be discussed in this chapter. Companies have begun to realize that CMPs must move beyond the crisis team to include all members of an organization. Companies can be held legally liable if they lack proper crisis planning. The expanded role of crisis management will be considered. Finally, the need to integrate private sector and government crisis preparedness is considered. This discussion includes a short explanation of the government's mandated National Incident Management System (NIMS) because you might encounter this system during a large-scale crisis.

DEVELOPING A CRISIS MANAGEMENT PLAN

I have trained many individuals on how to write a CMP. It is not a difficult process, but it does require focus. This section reviews the parts of a CMP and the process for drafting one. Ideally the crisis management team is involved in developing the plan. As a result, I begin the discussion of the CMP with a look at crisis teams.

Crisis Teams

The crisis team is the group of people who will manage the organization's response to the crisis. Crisis teams typically are composed of people from the following functional areas: legal, security, operations/technical, safety, public relations, quality assurance, financial, and a representative of the CEO. The functional selection of crisis team members is driven by the need to have certain knowledge (i.e., legal and operations), skills (i.e., public relations), and power (e.g., representative of the CEO). You want people on the crisis team who have the knowledge and skills necessary to combat a crisis.[1]

I would add one more person to the team: the full-time crisis manager/head of the crisis management unit. For crisis management to be part of the organization's DNA, there must be a full-time crisis manager. She or he should be part of every crisis team and in most cases runs the team. The crisis manager should be charged by the CEO to make the decisions. The crisis manager should have the power to act on behalf of the CEO, making him or her the de facto representative of the CEO.

Another consideration for the crisis team should be personality traits. Certain personality traits work well in a crisis situation, and others do not. Preferred crisis team traits are the ability to handle stress, high tolerance for ambiguity, and low communication apprehension. When you ask crisis team members about the most important trait, their answer is the ability to handle stress. Crisis management requires fast action in pressurized situations and is not for everyone. One might be a great engineer but a bad crisis team member. Training is useful in weeding out people who cannot handle stress. Team members who crack during a drill will be of little value during an actual crisis.

We each have different levels of ambiguity tolerance or the ability to handle uncertainty. Crises are, by nature, ambiguous. Crises are considered information vacuums—the unknown that must be known. People with low ambiguity tolerance will feel increased stress and be less effective on a crisis team.

Communication apprehension is a fear of expressing your ideas to others. Team members are selected because they bring important knowledge and skill to the team. If a person is reluctant to speak, his or her contributions are lost.[2] Again, training will help sort out who really belongs on the team. This point will be developed further in the section on training.

The Crisis Management Plan

The CMP is not a step-by-step guide on how to handle a crisis. There is no way such a plan can be drafted; do not be convinced if someone says they can create such a plan for your organization. A CMP is a carefully arranged selection of information that can aid a crisis team. President Dwight Eisenhower once said, "Plans are useless, but planning is indispensable." That quotation captures the value of the CMP. The CMP does not tell you how to manage a crisis but rather highlights what should be done when managing a crisis.

Time is a valuable commodity in a crisis. A CMP saves time during a crisis. The CMP precollects some critical information for easy access and makes some decisions by predetermining many responsibilities and tasks. The collected information includes contact information for people who may be needed during a crisis. Time is not wasted trying to figure out who to contact and how to reach them. You know that during a crisis certain tasks will need to be performed. Team members can be preassigned responsibilities for dealing with fundamental tasks, such as the news media or contacting specific people. When responsibilities and tasks are preassigned for fundamental crisis tasks, time is not lost making these basic decisions.

Speed and haste can cause people to make errors. The CMP provides reminders of what typically needs to be done during a crisis. Of course, the exact actions are modified to fit the specific crisis facing the organization. One important concern is documenting the actions of the crisis team. Documentation is useful when evaluating the performance of the crisis team and will serve as evidence if a lawsuit follows the crisis. The CMP will contain forms to remind the crisis team to document actions and provide guidance for collecting the information needed for the documentation.

TABLE 6.1:
GENERIC COMPONENTS OF A CRISIS MANAGEMENT PLAN

1. Cover Page
2. Introduction
3. Acknowledgments
4. Rehearsal Dates
5. Crisis Management Team List
6. CMT Contact Sheet
7. Secondary Contact Sheet
8. Crisis Risk Assessment
9. CMT Strategy Worksheet
10. Stakeholder Contact Worksheet
11. Business Continuity Plan Reference
12. Crisis Control Center
13. Postcrisis Evaluation Tools

CMPs can have various configurations. This section outlines a generic CMP that can be adapted for your organization. Table 6.1 lists the basic elements of the generic CMP. Appendix A contains samples of select elements. A CMP begins with a series of official pages: cover page, introduction, acknowledgments, and rehearsal dates. These serve to make people aware of the value of the plan. The cover page identifies the document as the CMP, notes whether the document is confidential, and lists the date of the last revision. The introduction contains a message from the CEO that reinforces the importance of crisis management and the CMP. The acknowledgments page is completed by individuals on the crisis team and then returned to human resources. The form states the person has read and understands the CMP. The introduction and acknowledgments reinforce the importance and the seriousness of crisis management. Rehearsal dates lists each time training occurred and the type of training involved.

The next section of the CMP contains the contact information. The crisis management team (CMT) page lists the team members, their basic responsibilities, when the CMP should be activated (what is a crisis), and how to activate the CMP. The contact sheet has all possible contact information for the CMT members and their alternates. It is important to have alternates if a team member is unavailable. The secondary contact sheet is a list of people that might be needed during a crisis, such as the insurance company or a federal regulator.

The final section is composed of documentation materials and reminders. The crisis risk assessment was discussed in chapter 5. It involves identifying and rating the various crisis risks faced by an organization. You would place a table summary of your crisis risk assessment in the CMP for documentation purposes. The incident report is a record of what was done during the crisis. Key points include when the crisis was first discovered, where it happened, and when various people were contacted. The CMT strategy worksheet records all the statements personnel from the organization make about the crisis to external stakeholders. The messages are listed along with the target stakeholder(s) for each message and the objective of the message. The worksheet also contains a list of technical terms that might need to be translated for stakeholders. This prevents a jargon-laden message from confusing stakeholders.

The stakeholder contact worksheet records when a stakeholder makes a request for information, who the stakeholder is, how the organization responded, and when the organization delivered the response. Often in a crisis, the team does not have the answer to a question and promises to answer it later. The stakeholder contact worksheet allows the team to track requests and to make sure the promised follow-up is delivered. The business continuity plan (BCP) is a reminder that the company may take action to ensure that business as usual is maintained. The BCP is a separate document. However, the BCP may call for changes that the crisis team will need to account for in its actions.

The crisis control center is the physical location where the crisis team will meet. This may be a dedicated room or just a conference room. Alternative sites need to be included in case the primary crisis control center was destroyed or is inaccessible. The postcrisis evaluation tools are a series of interview questions and surveys that can be adapted for the postmortem on the crisis management effort. Crises are a valuable learning experience, but no learning occurs without reflection. The postcrisis evaluation tools provide guidance for learning from the crisis.

The cover page includes the date of the last revision. A CMP should be updated significantly at least annually. Substantive updates are needed to incorporate changes that were recommended by previous exercise evaluations. Organizations and personnel change. This means the company's risks may have changed, contact people have changed, and/or contact information has changed. Crisis managers should continually update contact information and names for the CMP. Any changes in personnel or contact information can be sent and added to an existing plan. There is no need to reprint the entire CMP for contact information updates.

USING THE CMP: TRAINING THROUGH EXERCISES

Crisis training is best accomplished through exercises. An exercise is a practice activity that places organizational members in a simulated crisis event. The simulated events require the organizational members to perform the functions/tasks that would be expected of them in a real crisis.[3] Exercises are used to evaluate an organization's ability to execute all or part of a CMP. There are a variety of exercise types that an organization can use to test its capabilities. The benefits of exercising will be discussed, followed by an explanation of the various exercise options.

Benefits of Exercising CMPs

An exercise benefits both individual training as people practice their roles as well as system improvement as organizations improve their responses. Exercises can reveal weaknesses in a CMP, clarify roles and responsibilities, improve organizational coordination and communication, improve individual performance, and identify individual weaknesses. Practice does produce results.

As noted earlier, exercises can identify people who should not be members of the crisis team. Consider these two examples. During one exercise, a manager physically attacked one of the people helping run the exercise. Security had to remove the manager. In another simulation, a highly skilled manager sat quietly, staring into space. He simply stopped communicating with others. Both team members showed dysfunctional behavior in crisis exercises and were removed from the team. Research shows that how people act in an exercise is how they will respond in a crisis.[4] Better to find the weak links before rather than during a crisis.

In July 1989, United Airlines Flight 232 crashed during a failed landing attempt in Sioux City, Iowa. The disaster claimed 109 lives, but 189 passengers survived. Preparation and practice saved lives on Flight 232. In 1987, Sioux City had conducted a full-scale exercise involving the crash of a commercial airliner. The exercise revealed a number of problems with their CMP, including confused communication between units and inadequate equipment needs including a shortage of ambulances. Actions were taken after the exercise to correct the problems. After postmortem/crisis evaluation, officials noted that the mistakes they made in the exercise did not happen during the actual crisis.[5]

The Sioux City example points to a critical part of exercises— learning. The organization's performance must be carefully analyzed after an exercise. CMPs and personnel must be scrutinized. A series of tough questions must be asked and answered. Which parts of the CMP worked and which did not? Did the CMP miss something important? How did each crisis team member perform? Who would benefit from additional training? Who should be replaced on the crisis team? Exercises are pointless if no effort is made to learn from them.

Types of Exercises

Exercises are built around functions. Functions are actions or tasks that must be performed during a crisis. Table 6.2 provides the Federal Emergency Management Agency's (FEMA) list of thirteen functions in emergency management. What functions would you identify for your crisis team? Clearly FEMA's list focuses on the city level, but the key ideas can apply to organizations. For instance,

TABLE 6.2: EMERGENCY MANAGEMENT FUNCTIONS
1. Alert Notification (Emergency Response)
2. Warning (Public)
3. Communications
4. Coordination and Control
5. Emergency Public Information
6. Damage Assessment
7. Health and Medical
8. Individual/Family Assistance
9. Public Safety
10. Public Works/Engineering
11. Transportation
12. Resource Management
13. Continuity of Government

FEMA is concerned about continuity of government, whereas organizations are concerned with the continuity of business. Use the FEMA list as a guide when you develop your list of functions for crisis management. Exercises are then developed to test one or more functions.

There are five types of exercises: orientation seminar, drill, tabletop exercises, functional exercise, and full-scale exercise. The types of exercises are organized according to complexity. Organizations should work their way up to a full-scale exercise, not start with one. Mastering the more basic exercises builds confidence and the skills necessary to tackle the more complex exercises.

Orientation Seminar

An orientation seminar provides an overview to the crisis management process. People learn the CMP, their roles, the procedures to be followed, and equipment to be used. Participants should be encouraged to ask questions about the assignment of responsibilities and how actions will be coordinated. A CMP only saves time when people know what they should do (responsibilities, procedures, and coordination). The orientation helps people understand what they and other team members should be doing during crisis. An orientation exercise is run in a conference room and lasts one to two hours.

Drill

A drill is a coordinated and supervised exercise that tests one crisis management function. A drill does not try to coordinate between units, nor does it require activation of the crisis management center. The focus is on just one aspect of the crisis management process. For instance, a drill could highlight employee notification or the evaluation of hazardous chemical release. Equipment may be needed if the function requires the use of equipment such as warning systems or containment materials. The drill can be conducted on site and usually lasts thirty minutes to two hours.

Tabletop Exercise

A tabletop exercise is a guided analysis of a crisis situation. *Guided* means there is a facilitator who controls the flow of information to participants. The tabletop simulates a real crisis, and information is revealed over time just as in a real crisis. The participants are given a description of the problem at the start. The facilitator provides information in response to questions from the crisis team. The team is not spoon-fed information; they must work for it. The tabletop exercise is supposed to be low stress and informal. The exercise is conducted in a large conference room, and team members talk through what they would do. The team practices its decision-making skills guided by the CMP. A tabletop exercise can help spot holes or weaknesses in the CMP and the team members' skills. A tabletop will run around four hours, although it can be longer.

Functional Exercise

The functional exercise is a simulated interactive exercise that tests capabilities through a response to a simulated crisis. The functional exercise is time-pressured. Facilitators keep the simulation moving in real times. The team cannot simply talk through ideas as it would in a tabletop exercise. The crisis unfolds in real time, and the crisis team must keep pace. The focus is on the coordination, integration, and interaction of crisis policies, procedures, and personnel. The facilitators control the messages/information received by the team. The messages can be a response to what the crisis team has done and/or the release of information timed to match when such information might be known in a crisis. A functional exercise requires the use of the crisis command center. People need to be where they would be during a crisis and use the same equipment. A functional exercise will last from four to eight hours depending on the nature of the crisis.

There are different types of facilitators. A controller manages and directs the exercise. Some facilitators are players. This means they play the roles of the people the crisis team needs to contact, such as local fire officials or federal officials. Other facilitators are designed as evaluators. Their role is only to observe and evaluate; they do not communicate to anyone during the exercise. Does this sound elaborate? It should, because a functional exercise is elaborate. I have participated in a few such exercises, and they are amazing with how messages and events are timed within the crisis scenario and how players enact their roles. A company can develop its own functional exercise. It will take roughly six to eighteen months to prepare a functional exercise. Another option is to hire consultants who specialize in delivering realistic functional exercises. You pay others to prepare the exercise instead of creating your own, running the exercise, and evaluating the performance of the CMT. If you plan to create your own, I recommend sitting through a few functional exercises to get a feel for the process and the types of materials required for a realistic experience.

Full-Scale Exercise

The full-scale exercise is the ultimate in crisis experience. It simulates a real crisis as closely as possible, including taking action in the field. The difference with a drill is that equipment is really deployed and other actions are really taken in a full-scale exercise, rather than just saying something was done. People don't merely report what they would do, they actually do it. There is not just a command to deploy fire suppression; people and equipment are deployed. It is not just a report that there are ten accident victims; there are ten people with simulated injuries. Moreover, a full-scale drill requires coordination with other entities, such as local emergency responders. Someone does not simply play the role of the fire chief; the fire chief is there. The Sioux City exercise was a full-scale exercise. It will take a year or more to prepare a full-scale exercise. Part of that time is spent coordinating with the external entities. Again, you may wish to hire someone to help you develop and implement a full-scale exercise. A full-scale exercise will run one or more days.[6]

All five exercise types require evaluation if the organization is to learn from them. Even orientation sessions can reveal gaps in a CMP, such as clarity of roles and responsibilities in a crisis. If your organization has never conducted an exercise, start small and build from there. However, you should have at least one functional exercise per year. Only the functional and full-scale exercises supply the stress that will help identify problem team members. The functional exercise should correspond to revisions in the CMP. The exercise will test the new and improved CMP. Never let a real crisis be the time that a new or revised CMP is tested. Companies beta test products for a reason. The same logic applies to CMPs. Full-scale exercises will be conducted every few years. They are too labor-intensive to conduct annually but are an important step in building connections between the public and private sectors for crisis management, a topic that will be addressed in the next section. Work with local emergency personnel to help develop a schedule for full-scale exercises. You might be able to work with their mandated requirements to complete full-scale exercises for emergency management training.

IMPORTANT TRENDS IN CMP AND EXERCISES

There are two trends involving CMPs and training that should continue: expanding some training to all employees and public–private cooperation. Both trends expand crisis thinking and increase the number of people who are prepared for a crisis. Increased preparation should lead to reduced injuries and loss of life during a crisis.

All Employees

The discussion of the exercises focused on the crisis team. Except for full-scale exercises, only the crisis team members and perhaps a few other select employees are involved. All employees may be at risk during a crisis. Explosions, fires, and chemical releases can place entire facilities at risk. The events of September 11, 2001, made companies more aware of the need to prepare all employees for crises. As noted earlier, companies might be legally liable if they do not. This is when a drill exercise is handy. Drills can include all employees and test the following skills: evacuation, shelter in place, and use of safety equipment.

The Department of Homeland Security is actively trying to get all Americans to prepare for emergencies. Included in this effort are companies. Do your employees know how to get out of the facility? Do your employees know what to do after they evacuate? Is there an assembly point and means of accounting for people? Companies are encouraged to review and to practice evacuation plans. Every company should develop and practice a site-specific evacuation plan that covers all employees. This is much like the fire drills we all went through in grade school. Practice does help. The reason the loss of life was not greater on September 11 is that companies in the World Trade Center towers had practiced evacuation plans after the earlier bombing.

Some crises require employees to shelter in place. There are times when it is not safe to go outside, and workers should stay inside.

Employees need to understand and be able to implement a shelter-in-place plan. The employees must be urged to stay inside and the building sealed off from outside air. Personnel must act to shut off the cooling, heating, and ventilation systems, signs need to be displayed that signal a shelter in place, doors should be sealed with duct tape, windows and vents should be covered with plastic, and sign-in sheets should be circulated and tallied. Employees not involved with the crisis team can have responsibilities for helping seal off the building. Exercises will help all employees know what they should do during a shelter-in-place event. The federal government recommends that two shelter-in-place drills be conducted per year.[7]

Part of preparedness is being properly equipped. Recommended equipment includes plastic sheets precut for windows and vents, flashlights with fresh batteries, battery-operated radios, duct tape, water, food, and first-aid kits. Many companies now provide employees with respirators, including escape hoods or gas masks. The federal government supports the purchase of respirators.[8] Guidelines should be provided on how to use the equipment. It also is important to conduct drills to test how well employees can use the key equipment. The emergency preparedness aspect of crisis management must extend to all employees and include all drills.

Public–Private Cooperation

As noted in the discussion of full-scale exercises, some crises require coordination between the organization and emergency responders from the community. Every community is required by law to have a community emergency operation plan (EOP). An EOP is much like a CMP. It is very possible that a company's crisis will affect the community or a community's crisis will affect a company. Generally organizations and communities do little to coordinate their plans and responses. The private and public sides must practice together if coordination is to work. Only through exercises will the two sides learn how to integrate their responses.[9]

I worked on crisis training for a large manufacturer. The company included local government officials in the training sessions to promote cooperation. The private–public barrier needs to disappear. When companies work with community responders, the company benefits. The community responders are better prepared and perhaps better equipped to help the company. Chemical companies have been known to supply local responders with haz-mat equipment that the responders could not afford but might need when responding to a chemical-related crisis at one of their facilities. The equipment could be used for other community-related crises as well. This offers a perfect illustration of the value of private–public cooperation in crisis management.

Government Regulation

Okay, I said two trends, so what is this third topic? The Department of Homeland Security, with advice from FEMA, has developed best practices for handling disasters/crises. The best practice is known as the National Incident Management System (NIMS). As of March 2004, all state, local, tribal, and federal governments are to use NIMS. The idea should improve efficiency and effectiveness when teams from different levels of government must coordinate their efforts. NIMS is a refinement of the incident command structure FEMA and other public responders have been using for years. Table 6.3 lists the components of NIMS.

The NIMS National Integration Center was established to help governments learn and be certified for NIMS. Part of this effort is an online training course offered free of charge by FEMA. So what does this have to do with your company? Private companies do not need to be NIMS certified or to use the NIMS system in their own crisis management efforts. However, if your company becomes part of a community-based crisis, NIMS will be in use. It is useful for crisis managers to be familiar with NIMS just in case their crisis draws them under the NIMS umbrella. Appendix B provides government documentation that describes NIMS. NIMS can be found on the Internet at www.fema.gov/nims.

TABLE 6.3:
COMPONENTS OF NATIONAL INCIDENT MANAGEMENT SYSTEM

1. Command and Management
2. Preparation
3. Resource Management
4. Communication and Information Management
5. Supporting Technologies
6. Ongoing Management and Maintenance

SUMMARY

Exercises separate crisis management as DNA verses crisis management as an add-on function. The foundation of crisis management is the careful selection of a team and the thoughtful preparation of a CMP. Exercises bring the CMP to life and test the mettle of the plan and the crisis team. It also reinforces the organization's commitment to crisis management. Exercises, especially functional and full-scale exercises, require a commitment of personnel and financial resources. Having one functional exercise per year is a strong step toward crisis management as DNA. Reinforcing the functional exercise with evacuation and shelter-in-place drills further strengthens the organization's preparedness and commitment. The team should have at least one member who is a full-time crisis manager that reports directly to the CEO. This professional crisis manager should lead the team when things go haywire. A full-time crisis manager who has the power to make decisions is yet another sign that crisis management is becoming part of the organization's DNA.

7

●\

Crisis Management as DNA: Overcoming Resistance to the Crisis Management Process

●\

A large corporation announces a major change initiative for several hundred managers in the organization. A series of kickoff events are held, including inspirational speeches from top executives. Managers are sent large binders, pamphlets, and video tapes. The material sat on their shelves and collected dust.[1] Do you think this change was a success? Like most change efforts in corporations, it met an unfortunate demise. Your crisis management plan will be the next binder collecting dust if the crisis management process is not carefully integrated into the organizational culture and made part of the organization's DNA. For crisis management to be in the organizational DNA, there needs to be constant monitoring of threats, regular updates of the plan, and annual drills. The crisis management process is more than a plan in a binder.

When you consider the organizational crises that have been featured in the news media, it seems rational for an organization to develop and use crisis management. Why not use policies and procedures that would make your organization safer and more effective? Unfortunately, a common refrain you hear from people trying to establish crisis management in an organization is "resistance." Organizations are nothing more that a collection of individuals. As a result, organizations can be irrational and avoid doing things that are good for them. People drive too fast in the rain and eat fatty foods. So why shouldn't an organization reject crisis management? When you attempt to integrate crisis management into an organization, expect resistance and plan for ways to overcome it. This chapter examines why people resist changes, such as a crisis management process, and strategies for overcoming the resistance and integrating crisis management into an organization's DNA.

WHY PEOPLE RESIST

Generally, people do not like change. Making crisis management a part of your organizational DNA requires change. People will take on new roles, learn new skills, and have new responsibilities. Change resistance has both an individual and an organizational component. On an individual level, we resist for two reasons: (1) anxiety over the unknown and (2) inconvenience. A crisis management program represents something different. It isn't the same, comfortable routine.[2] You are learning new information and skills. Can you really learn and execute them? New information, roles, and ways of doing things can create doubt because they are unknown. Change is also inconvenient because people need to alter schedules. You need to go to meetings about crisis management and be part of the training. It adds to the list of the many things you already need to do.

The organizational component involves the organization's history of change. Does the organization have a record of trying new things and then abandoning them? Past change failures lead to fatigue and cynicism; employees do not believe the organization can make the change either because of a lack of managerial skill or desire. Why invest time and effort in yet another fad that management will soon abandon? You can actually measure cynicism about organizational change in a company. It might be worth finding out the level of cynicism about organizational change in your organization before trying to make crisis management part of the organization's DNA. Crisis management is an extremely tough sell when you combine individual resistance to change with an organizational cynicism about change. Table 7.1 provides a list of questions you can use to assess the level of cynicism for change that exists in your organization.

The negative reaction to change typically follows a four-stage pattern. This pattern will help you develop strategies for overcoming

> ### TABLE 7.1:
> ### QUESTIONS FOR CYNICISM ABOUT ORGANIZATION CHANGE
>
> ---
>
> How would your employees answer these statements?
>
> 1. The people responsible for making improvements do not know enough about what they are doing.
> 2. The people responsible for making changes do not have the skills needed to do their jobs.
> 3. Plans for future improvements will not amount to much.
> 4. Suggestions on how to solve problems will not produce much real change.
> 5. Attempts to make things better will not produce good results.
> 6. The people responsible for making changes around here do not have the resources they need to get the job done.
>
> If you think employees would agree with these statements, you have cynicism about organizational change.

resistance. The first step is denial: "This change is never going to happen." Again, past failures make this reaction even stronger. The second step is anger: "Why do I have to do this?" People are angry because you are making them face the unknown and disrupting their routines. The third step is bargaining: "Okay, but let's do it this way." People try to alter the plans to better suit their needs. The fourth step is acceptance: "All right, I'll do it." People verbally agree to try the change. These four steps will be useful when we discuss strategies for making crisis management part of the organizational culture.

It is wrong to assume that change efforts fail simply because of resistance. Although resistance is natural, it is not the only reason changes fail. Two other reasons for change failure are poor design and poor communication. Poor design is a failure of the change team to develop a plan for making the change part of the organization. Systems need to change (a point we will return to shortly) for a change to work. Poor communication is a failure to fully explain the change (what it is and its implications) to those affected by it. Employees are much more willing to be involved in and support a change when they feel they have received quality information about it.[3] Understanding why change can fail will better prepare you for making the crisis management change work in your organization.

WORKING TOWARD ACCEPTANCE OF
CRISIS MANAGEMENT

Because crisis management is a change, a careful, strategic approach is needed. In general, you need to build a core of support and expand from there. The primary phase involves creating your core of supporters; the secondary phase involves spreading the word.

Primary Phase

Any discussion of organizational change recommends using powerful people in your organization to vocally support the change.[4] Every organization has prime movers, powerful people in the organization to whom employees look for guidance. You need prime movers to champion the crisis management change. The CEO, the CFO, and any other influential members of management or even support staff can be effective champions. Another target for your core change unit will be people who will have important roles in the crisis management change.[5] You want their buy-in early so they are dedicated when the time comes for them to actually make the plan come to life. Early involvement in the process will give employees a sense of ownership for the crisis management change that will translate into greater commitment to it.

Identifying the people for your core is the easy part. The hard part is persuading them to be part of the crisis management change effort. You will have to sell the need for crisis management if you are asking them to commit time and energy. In the primary phase, the message needs to emphasize the benefits of crisis management. In particular, you need to establish the problem that exists with the status quo. How does the lack of a crisis management process place your organization and stakeholders at risk? You need to make people dissatisfied with the current state of the organization.[6]

The message should be driven by a vision—what the future would look like with the change. You should emphasize how the organization and employees will be better off with the crisis management process in place. The vision should be realistic. Don't promise what the plan cannot deliver. Although the crisis management process can help prevent many crises, it cannot guarantee 100 percent eradication. The crisis management process can better protect people and resources but not prevent all injuries or losses. The vision will help create a sense of purpose and urgency because people in the core unit will know what you are trying to accomplish.

To support the vision, you will need to create talking points. The talking points support the need for the crisis management change— providing a rationale for the change. The talking points explain how the crisis management process will make the vision of improving the organization a reality. You provide people with reasons to accept the crisis management change and reinforce the sense of urgency. Focus on the question "Why?"

An effective starting point for the talking points are the risks/ crisis types your organization faces. Many people choose to ignore the fact that bad things can happen. Make people face the reality of the various crises that could hit your organization. Again, be realistic in the list of crises. Focus on a few of the most likely crisis types instead of trying to provide an exhaustive list. Discussing the crisis types highlights the current vulnerabilities of your organization. Note how current practices fall well short of being prepared for these threats. The status quo is not good enough. These crises can occur and the organization is not ready to handle them. You basically create a sense of fear. Fear can be a motivator for change. However, people need to believe the threat is real and that there is a way to reduce the threat. Reinforce your points by providing examples of actual crises suffered by other organizations in your industry. The examples reinforce the point that crises do occur in your industry and provide a sense of realism. If it happened to them, it can happen to us.

Your next challenge is to explain how the crisis management process helps reduce the threat/fear. The message should include what is involved in a crisis management process and not just simply focusing on a crisis management plan. You are selling crisis management as DNA, not as a binder that collects dust. Focus on how a crisis management process should reduce crises, injuries and deaths, financial damage, and reputational damage. This part of your message emphasizes the benefits of the crisis management process. Think of the talking points as two parts: (1) the threat from current practices and (2) the benefits from having a crisis management process. The threat helps create a sense of dissatisfaction with the status quo, and the information about the crisis management process helps establish a way to be satisfied.

Talking points are designed to synthesize the central ideas. You are not writing a fifteen-minute speech or ten-page report on the value of the crisis management process. You have to refine your ideas into a few points that you can deliver quickly. It should be a message you can convincingly deliver in three minutes or less. You might want to print up a small card that summarizes your talking points. Distribute cards to people you talk with so they have something to remember or refer to when they are asked about the crisis management change. Once your core unit is in place, you are ready to spread the crisis management message throughout the organization. You will be using planning and communication to overcome resistance and win change acceptance.

Secondary Phase

Ideally, you want everyone in the organization to be talking about the crisis management process. You are creating organizational buzz. People are talking about the possibility of instituting the crisis management process. The communication needs to be interactive or two-way. Not only is the core group using the talking points, they are soliciting feedback as well. People will have questions about a possible change and you must remain open to and answer the questions. Lack of listening to others is one of the main contributors to resisting change. People feel excluded from the process and un-sure of what is happening when their questions go unanswered. Quality information is information employees want, not what you think they need.[7] The opening example in this chapter used only one-way communication, a contributing factor to the failure.

You will need to flood the organization with your basic message. Take advantage of all the communication channels available to you. Crisis management messages should appear on the intranet, in memos and e-mail, as topics at departmental/divisional meetings, as items in newsletters, and on bulletin boards. Be sure your message remains consistent across the various channels and peo-ple promoting the crisis management process. This does not mean everyone says the same thing with the same language. What it does mean is that the central message is the same for all of the core members. Establishing a vision and talking points should help promote consistency in the message.

If the organization has an intranet, devote a section to the crisis management process. Outline the process and its benefits, provide a list of frequently asked questions, and provide a link people can use to e-mail questions. It would also be a good idea to hold an organizational town hall meeting to discuss the topic. The town hall format allows your core people to explain the crisis management process and to directly answer questions people might have. Focus on both sending messages and soliciting feedback/questions. Maybe ask people to submit ideas like potential crisis risks in their departments or how their department can contribute to the crisis-sensing network. Communication is much less effective when it is one-way. Two-way communication shows greater respect for people and allows the communicators to better understand and adjust to the concerns of the listener.

This is also the time to bring the skeletons out of the closet. If there were past change failures, talk about those failures. Explain why past efforts failed. This would include acknowledging past managerial mistakes or lack of commitment or resources. Your message is more credible when you deal openly with past failures. Use the previous failures as the foundation for future success. Explain what was learned from failures that will help make this change a success. People will remain cynical if they think the past will be repeated. They need a reason to believe this change will be different from prior failures. Do not try to hide or run from the past. Embrace it and use it to your advantage.

Keep in mind that one message does not fit all. You have the vision and talking points as a central message. However, you can tailor the message to the current stage of resistance. For those people in denial, it is important to note the positives and the negatives of the change. People tend to think they are being misled when only positives are given. Recognize that a real change can mean extra work for people. But explain how the positives outweigh the negatives—give them a reason to want the change. Do not ignore opposition or ridicule their concerns. You need to address opposing arguments. Ignoring it does not make the problem go away nor win over possible converts. You need to accept the reasons people give for resistance and try to replace them with reasons to support. Ridicule will reinforce resistance, not set the stage for acceptance.

When people are angry, you need to clarify the details of the change. How exactly will the crisis management process affect them and their jobs? You need to show that you understand their anger with the change. Accept the anger; do not try to deny it. Part of this is allowing people to vent. It may be unpleasant for you to listen to what may seem to be irrational complaints. But the person may just want to vent, and once they do the anger is dissipated, much like the customer who feels better after lecturing the customer service representative. The angry individual might just want someone to hear his or her problems, not solve them. It is the process that makes them feel better, not necessarily the outcome. Avoid escalating the conflict by getting into an argument or making threats. Do not take the anger personally. Acknowledge the concerns and restate your best reasons for the crisis management process.

When people are bargaining, be flexible on small matters. For instance, people may feel a certain time of year is better for a crisis drill than the one you have identified. Make that change if people will feel better. It is important to have a drill, not to have it on a specific date. However, know which points cannot be changed and hold firm on those. Not having drills is not an option. Keep reminding people of the long-term benefits of the crisis management process. Take all ideas under advisement. Avoid quick dismissals even if you know the idea cannot be used. You show respect for people by respecting their ideas.

Once the decision to implement the change occurs, praise people for their efforts. Avoid the temptation to gloat or joke about the past. The danger is to equate accepting a change with making a change work. If people are told they must be part of the crisis management process, they eventually accept it. However, that does not mean they actively support it, nor do they seek to make it work. You need to go beyond mere acceptance to commitment to a change. Commitment to change requires integration into the organizational culture, an important element of the change plan.

Integrating Change into the Organizational Culture

Just because a decision is made that an organization will make a change does not mean the change will be made successfully. It is useful to think of change as a seed. Like a seed, change in isolation will wither and die. The organization's culture provides the fertile soil for change to thrive. This lesson is essential when starting the crisis management process. It is very easy to draft a crisis management plan (including assignments to the crisis management team), place the plan in binders, and let the binder sit on bookshelves with other lifeless documents. The crisis management process needs to be a living part of the organization. A change becomes a part of the organization through its culture. This section reviews what culture is then discusses strategies for making the crisis management process part of the culture.

What Is Culture?

We often hear people talk about the culture of an organization but rarely define what they mean by culture. Moreover, different conceptualizations of culture exist. In general, we can think of culture as the way things are done in a particular organization. Culture is composed of the beliefs, values, and practices that are taken for granted but guide actions and sense-making in the organization. The culture guides how people in an organization think, act, and feel. Small adjustments to culture can be made that will allow a change to be viewed as part of the existing culture.[8] Change works best when it is incremental. For instance, the crisis management process is not revolutionary. It is consistent with how most organizations think about safety and risk management. As an agent of change, you need to find a place in the cultural soil for the crisis management process seed.

Integrating the Crisis Management Process into the Culture

It is helpful to think of modifying the culture as a four-step process. The first step is to assess your existing culture. Like a fish that does not know it is wet, we often cannot see our own organizational culture. Examine your organization to see what values and beliefs are important. Table 7.2 provides a list of common cultural indicators. Review these indicators as means of describing your organization's culture. The second step is to find a connection between the crisis management process and the existing culture. Determine how the crisis management process is consistent with existing values and beliefs. A natural connection to the existing culture makes the change easier to integrate into current practices. The crisis management process will require new procedures and policies, but these new elements should reflect central elements of the existing culture.

The third step is cultural reification. You need to make sure the crisis management process remains and does not fade from memory. This is the tricky part. Too often managers say the organization

TABLE 7.2: CULTURE INDICATORS
1. Reward systems
2. What management pays attention to
3. Stories, myths, and legends
4. Dominant beliefs and values
5. Decision-making
6. Issues that generate emotions
7. Physical layout of the business
8. Jokes
9. Language that is used
10. Practices that are ridiculed or revered by employees

has a crisis management plan somewhere. The CMP is probably on a shelf gathering dust. But people in the organization rarely, if ever, think about crisis management. Reification requires that the new policies and procedures related to crisis management be tied to rewards or punishments in an organization. This would include performance evaluations for personnel tied closely to the crisis management process. People are more likely to pay attention to policies and procedures that have a bite. If employees are evaluated on their ability to provide crisis-sensing information to the crisis manager and performance in the crisis drills, those behaviors take on much greater salience.

The fourth step is monitoring the change. You need to be sure that the early efforts are sustained in the organization.[9] Are the new crisis management policies being followed? Are the new appraisal systems in use? Are the rewards or punishments being delivered consistently? Returning to the metaphor of the seed, you need to make sure the young plant remains healthy and is getting the proper nourishment.

Final Warning

Integrating the crisis management process into the organization's culture is not a quick and easy task. It takes time, commitment, and a clear plan. You need to ask yourself if you have the passion and conviction required to make this change a reality. Although careful preparation will make your task easier, it is no guarantee of success. Organizations do not always embrace what is good for them.

Be prepared for the resistance and criticism that comes with promoting a change. Thicken your skin and try not to take it all personally.

SUMMARY

There is no doubt that having a crisis management process is beneficial to an organization. Oddly, the number one reason given for investing in a crisis management process is that an organization just experienced a crisis. The crisis served as a wake-up call. People engage in any number of risky behaviors they know are bad for them and avoid many they know are good for them. Organizations are no different. People will resist attempts to implement a crisis management process. Implementation can fall short if just having a crisis management plan is taken as a measure of success. Success can be declared when the organization regularly monitors risks and threats, exercises the crisis management plan at least annually, extends crisis thinking to safety drills for all employees, revises the crisis management plan regularly, and has at least one person dedicated full-time to overseeing crisis management. It takes commitment and a well-planned effort to make the crisis management process part of the organization's DNA. Hopefully this chapter will prove useful in guiding those efforts.

Appendix A

Sample Crisis Management Plan Elements

INCIDENT REPORT

Date and Time   Initial Report _____
   Incident was Reported:
Individual Reporting   Follow-up _____
   the Incident:
How to Contact the Reporting
   Individual:

Description of the Incident:

Exact Location of the Incident:

List the Personnel and Units Responding to the Incident:

Describe What is Being Done to Address the Incident and by
   Whom:

List Any Follow up Action that Is Needed:

Detail the Damage Inflicted by the Crisis:

Date and Time the Crisis Team Was Notified:

What Other Units (i.e., fire department, security,
   EMTs, etc.) Were Contacted and When?

CMT STRATEGY WORKSHEET

Stakeholder(s) Targeted by the Message:

- consider the status of the current relationship with each stakeholder
- review the primary organizational performance expectations of each stakeholder

List Stakeholder(s) Here:

Goal of the Message:

Attach a copy of the actual message to this sheet.

STAKEHOLDER CONTACT WORKSHEET

Date: Time:

Organizational Member Handling the Inquiry:

Channel Used to Contact the Organization:

Stakeholder's Classification (i.e., media, stockholder,
   community leader, etc.):

   Inquiring Person's Name and Title:

   Inquiring Person's Organizational Affiliation:

   How to Reach the Inquiring Person:

Question/Inquiry:

Response:

Any Follow-up Needed: If so, by when:

POSTCRISIS EVALUATION TOOLS

Sample introductory statement: At _____ we are constantly trying to improve our crisis management performance. Improvement requires a thorough review of our crisis management efforts. Your feedback is an important part of the evaluation. Please provide honest and complete answers to the following questions. If you wish, your answers will be anonymous, just skip the optional information section. Thank for your time and help with our evaluation process.

Optional Information

Name: Phone:

Department/Organization:

SAMPLE SURVEY ITEMS/INTERVIEW QUESTIONS

What role did you play in the crisis management process?

How did you learn about the crisis?

Were you satisfied with the crisis notification system?

   Why or why not?

How would you rate your unit's crisis management performance?

1	2	3	4	5
Very Poor	Poor	Average	Good	Excellent

How would you rate the organization's overall crisis management performance?

1	2	3	4	5
Very Poor	Poor	Average	Good	Excellent

Were you asked to supply information to the crisis team?

Was the request understandable?

  Why or why not?

Was the request reasonable?

  Why or why not?

What other suggestions do you have for improving the crisis
  management process?

SAMPLE SURVEY ITEMS/QUESTIONS FOR CRISIS TEAM
MEMBERS ONLY

Were you satisfied with the process the team used to collect
information?

   Why or why not?

Were you satisfied with how other organizational units
responded to the team's information requests?

   Why or why not?

Were you satisfied with how external stakeholders responded to
the team's information requests?

   Why or why not?

Which units/stakeholders were especially helpful?

Which units/stakeholders were especially problematic?

Appendix B

Department of Homeland Security Fact Sheet for NIMS

NIMS MAKES AMERICA SAFER, FROM OUR NATION TO OUR NEIGHBORHOODS

NIMS establishes standardized incident management processes, protocols, and procedures that all responders—federal, state, tribal, and local—will use to coordinate and conduct response actions. With responders using the same standardized procedures, they will all share a common focus, and will be able to place full emphasis on incident management when a homeland security incident occurs—whether terrorism or natural disaster. In addition, national preparedness and readiness in responding to and recovering from an incident is enhanced since all of the nation's emergency teams and authorities are using a common language and set of procedures.

ADVANTAGES OF NIMS

NIMS incorporates incident management best practices developed and proven by thousands of responders and authorities across America. These practices, coupled with consistency and national standardization, will now be carried forward throughout all incident management processes: exercises, qualification and certification, communications interoperability, doctrinal changes, training, and publications, public affairs, equipping, evaluating, and incident management. All of these measures unify the response community as never before.

NIMS WAS CREATED AND VETTED BY REPRESENTATIVES ACROSS AMERICA INCLUDING:

- Federal government,
- States,
- Territories,
- Cities, counties, and townships,
- Tribal officials,
- First responders.

KEY FEATURES OF NIMS:

- **Incident Command System (ICS).** NIMS establishes ICS as a standard incident management organization with five functional areas—command, operations, planning, logistics, and finance/administration—for management of all major incidents. To ensure further coordination, and during incidents involving multiple jurisdictions or agencies, the principle of unified command has been universally incorporated into NIMS. This unified command not only coordinates the efforts of many jurisdictions, but provides for and assures joint decisions on objectives, strategies, plans, priorities, and public communications.
- **Communications and Information Management.** Standardized communications during an incident are essential and NIMS prescribes interoperable communications systems for both incident and information management. Responders and managers across all agencies and jurisdictions must have a common operating picture for a more efficient and effective incident response.
- **Preparedness.** Preparedness incorporates a range of measures, actions, and processes accomplished before an incident

happens. NIMS preparedness measures include planning, training, exercises, qualification and certification, equipment acquisition and certification, and publication management. All of these serve to ensure that pre-incident actions are standardized and consistent with mutually-agreed doctrine. NIMS further places emphasis on mitigation activities to enhance preparedness. Mitigation includes public education and outreach, structural modifications to lessen the loss of life or destruction of property, code enforcement in support of zoning rules, land management, and building codes, and flood insurance and property buy-out for frequently flooded areas.

- **Joint Information System (JIS).** NIMS organizational measures enhance the public communication effort. The Joint Information System provides the public with timely and accurate incident information and unified public messages. This system employs Joint Information Centers (JIC) and brings incident communicators together during an incident to develop, coordinate, and deliver a unified message. This will ensure that federal, state, and local levels of government are releasing the same information during an incident.
- **NIMS Integration Center (NIC).** To ensure that NIMS remains an accurate and effective management tool, the NIMS NIC will be established by the Secretary of Homeland Security to assess proposed changes to NIMS, capture, and evaluate lessons learned, and employ best practices. The NIC will provide strategic direction and oversight of the NIMS, supporting both routine maintenance and continuous refinement of the system and its components over the long term. The NIC will develop and facilitate national standards for NIMS education and training, first responder communications and equipment, typing of resources, qualification and credentialing of incident management and responder personnel, and standardization of equipment maintenance and resources. The NIC will continue to use the collaborative process of federal, state, tribal, local, multi-discipline, and private authorities to assess prospective changes and assure continuity and accuracy.

Notes

CHAPTER 1

1. W. Timothy Coombs, *Ongoing Crisis Communication: Planning, Managing, and Responding* (Thousands Oaks, CA: Sage, 1999), 2–3; Laurence Barton, *Crisis in Organizations II* (Cincinnati, OH: Thompson Learning, 2001), 7–9.

2. "Burger King Recall of Pokemon Toy not Thorough Enough," Associated Press (28 Dec. 1999). *Lexis-Nexis Academic* (17 May 2005); "Burger King Ads to Warn about Toys," Associated Press (28 Jan. 2000). *Lexis-Nexis Academic* (17 May 2005); Gregg Cebrzynski, "Experts Say Pokemon Recall Unlikely to Tarnish Burger King's Image," *Nation's Restaurant News*, 34.2 (2000).

3. Kevin Poulsen, "Hacker Penetrates T-Mobile Systems," 11 Jan. 2005, online at www.securityfocus.com/news/10271 (accessed 12 May 2005).

4. W. Timothy Coombs, "West Pharmaceutical's Explosion: Structuring Crisis Discourse Knowledge," *Public Relations Review* 30 (2004): 467–473.

5. "Wendy's Doubles Chili Finger Reward to $100,000," Reuters, 5 April 2005, online at news.yahoo.com (accessed 15 May 2005);

"Woman in Wendy's Finger Case Arrested," Associated Press, 22 April 2005, online at www.forbes.com (accessed 12 May 2005).

6. Steven Fink, *Crisis Management: Planning for the Inevitable* (New York: American Management Association, 1986), 20–22.

7. Coombs, *Ongoing Crisis Communication*, 4.

8. Barton, 31–32; Coombs, *Ongoing Crisis Communication*, 83–84.

CHAPTER 2

1. "ChoicePoint: More ID Theft Warning," *CNNMoney*, 17 Feb. 2005, online at money.cnn.com (accessed 15 May 2005); Denise Potter, "Hackers Capture Info from George Mason U," *USA Today*, 11 Jan. 2005, online at www.usatoday.com (accessed 14 May 2005).

2. Martyn Williams, "Ebay, Amazon, Buy.com Hit by Attacks," IDG News Service, 9 Feb. 2000, online at www.nwfusion.com/news/2000/0209attack.html (accessed 15 May 2005); Corey Grice, "How a Basic Attack Crippled Yahoo," 7 Feb. 2000, online at news.com (accessed 15 May 2005).

3. Ellen Messmer, "The Anti-DDoS Prescription," *Network World*, 24 Sept. 2001, online at www.networkworld.com/buzz2001/anti ddos (accessed 14 May 2005).

4. "Security Breach Could Affect 500,00 People Nation-Wide," Continuity e-Guide, 23 Feb. 2005, online at disaster-resource.com (accessed 15 May 2005).

5. Potter, para. 7.

6. "Insider Threat Study: Computer System Sabotage in Critical Infrastructure Sectors," CERT, May 2005, online at www.cert.org/archive/pdf/insidercross051105.pdf (accessed 21 June 2005).

7. Ted Bridis, "Study Examines Motives for Office Sabotage," Miami Herald, 17 May 2005, online at www.miami.com (accessed 21 June 2005); D. Ian Hopper, "Technology: Hacking up, Disclosure down, FBI Survey," Web Pro Wire, 7 April 2002, online at www.webprowire.com/summaries/62059.html (accessed 14 May 2005).

8. Bridis, para. 7.

9. Kathy Macdonald, "A New Frontier in Crime...Identity Theft," in *The Future Is Convergence: 2005 West Proceedings*, ed.

Contingency Planning Management (Flemington, NJ: Witter, 2005), 173–184.

10. Alex Gramling, "Spread of Internet Lies Spooks Large Organizations," *New York Times*, 28 May 1997, online at www.alexgramling.net/nytimes.htm (accessed 12 June 2005).

11. Susana Enriquez and Donna Horowitz, "Finger Has Lunch Crowd Rethinking Its Choices," *Los Angeles Times*, 26 March 2005, sec. B, p. 1.

12. Catherine Tierney, "Workplace Shootings," *St. Louis Post-Dispatch*, 3 July 2003, sec. A, p. 7.

13. Lockheed Martin, "Lockheed Martin Statement Regarding Shooting Incident at Meridian, Mississippi Subassembly Plant," 8 July 2003, online at lockheedmartin.com (accessed 12 September 2003).

14. Ed Devlin, "A Top Consultant Discusses the Bombing of the World Trade Center," *Disaster Recovery Journal* 6.2 (1993), online at www.drj.com/special/wtc/w2_036.htm (accessed 12 June 2005); Anne M. McCarthy, "No Plan, No Site, No Business," *Disaster Recovery Journal* 6.2 (1993), online at www.drj.com/special/wtc/w2_033.htm (accessed 12 June 2005).

CHAPTER 3

1. W. Timothy Coombs and Sherry J. Holladay, "Helping Crisis Managers Protect Reputational Assets: Initial Tests of the Situational Crisis Communication Theory," *Management Communication Quarterly* 16 (2002): 176–181.

2. "Judge OKs Rules for Hepatitis Claims," *Charleston Daily Mail*, 13 Dec. 2003, sec. C, p. 5.

3. "Judge OKs Rules," 5; Paula Reed Ward, "Restaurant Needs Help on Image, Experts Say," *Pittsburgh Post-Gazette*, 14 Nov. 2003, sec. A, p. 1.

4. "Reports of Blindness in Men Using Viagra, Cialis," *MSNBC*, 27 May 2005, online at www.msnbc.com (accessed 27 May 2005).

5. "Patient Safety," *Heart Disease Weekly*, 31 Oct. 2004, 196.

6. Kerry Dooley and Kristen Hallam, "Merck Stock Plummets on Vioxx Report," *National Post's Financial Post & FP Investing*, 2 Nov. 2004, 8.

7. "Response to Article by Juni et al. Published in *The Lancet* on Nov. 5," Merck, 7 Nov. 2004, online at www.merck.com (accessed 10 Nov. 2004).

8. "Safety Recall," NESCO/American Harvest, 6 Nov. 2003, online at www.nesco.com/safety_recall (accessed 12 Nov. 2003).

9. "Chi-Chi's, Inc. Comments on the Dismissal of Three Lawsuits," Chi-Chi's, 1 Dec. 2003, online at www.chi-chis.com/pressrelease.htm (accessed 12 Jan. 2004).

10. "Bill Zavertnik," Chi-Chi's, 22 Nov. 2003, online at www.chi-chis.com/pressrelease.htm) (accessed 1 Dec. 2003).

11. "Preliminary Findings Confirms Blast at West Pharamaceutical Services in Kinston, NC Was a Dust Explosion," U.S. Chemical Safety Board, 18 June 2003, online at www.chemsafety.gov/news/2003/n20030602.htm (access 31 July 2003).

12. "Temporary Relocation," West Pharmaceuticals, 21 Feb. 2003, online at investor.westpharma.org (accessed 21 July 2003).

13. "Update," West Pharmaceuticals, 4 Feb. 2003, online at investor.westpharma.com (accessed 21 July 2003).

14. "Comments on Plant Explosion," West Pharmaceuticals, 29 Jan. 2003, online at investor.westpharma.com (accessed 21 July 2003).

15. "Provides Update," West Pharmaceuticals, 30 Jan. 2003, online at investor.westpharma.com (accessed 21 July 2003).

16. "Memorial Service," West Pharmaceuticals, 20 Feb. 2003, online at investor.westpharma.com (accessed 21 July 2003).

17. Emery P. Dalesio, "Investigators Look at Dust Build-up, Unknown Spark in Factory Blast," Associated Press, 4 Feb. 2003, online at www.ap.org (accessed 8 Feb. 2003).

18. Grahame Dowling, *Creating Corporate Reputations: Identity, Image, and Performance* (New York: Oxford University Press, 2001), 53.

19. "McDonald's Chairman and CEO Jim Cantalupo Passes Away," McDonald's Corporation, 19 May 2004, online at www.mcdonalds.com (accessed 20 June 2005).

20. "McDonald's Board of Directors Elects Charlie Bell President and CEO; Andrew J. McKenna Elected Non-Executive Chairman," McDonald's Corporation, 19 May 2004, online at www.mcdonalds.com (accessed 20 June 2005).

21. Sally J. Ray, *Strategic Communication in Crisis Management: Lessons from the Airline Industry* (Westport, CN: Quorum Books, 1999), 9–12.

22. Ray, 117–134.

23. "NTSB Concludes TWA Flight 800 Probe," CBS, 4 Aug. 2000, online at www.cbsnews.com (accessed 20 July 2005).

24. Ray, 117–134.

25. "Babe Star Arrested at Wendy's Protest," PETA, 3 July 2001, online at www.peta.org/feat/wendys/warnshot.html (accessed 18 June 2005).

26. "PETA Wins 'Wicked Wendy's' Campaign," PETA, 6 Sept. 2001, online at www.peta.org/news/newsitem.asp?id=360 (accessed 18 June 2005).

27. "Southern Baptists Vote for Disney Boycott," CNN, 18 June 1997, online at www.cnn.com (accessed 20 June 2005).

28. Robert L. Heath, "Public Relations," in *Encyclopedia of Public Relations*, ed. Robert L. Heath (Thousand Oaks, CA: Sage, 2005), 679–684.

CHAPTER 4

1. W. Timothy Coombs and Sherry J. Holladay, "Reasoned Action in Crisis Communication: An Attribution Theory-Based Approach to Crisis Management," in *Responding to Crisis: A Rhetorical Approach to Crisis Communication*, eds. Dan P. Millar and Robert L. Heath (Mahwah, NJ: Lawrence Erlbaum, 2004), 112.

2. Simon Willis, Laura Swanson, Luxman Satchi, and Kevin Thompson, "Design Defects of the Ford Pinto Gas Tank," online at www.fordpinto.com/blowup.htm (accessed 25 May 2005).

3. Francis T. Cullen, William Maakestad, and Gary Cavender, *Corporate Crime under Attack: The Ford Pinto Case and Beyond* (Cincinnati, OH: Anderson, 1987).

4. National Transportation Safety Board, "Loss of Pitch Control Caused Crash of Fatal Airliner Crash in Charlotte, North Carolina Last Year," 26 Feb. 2004, online at www.ntsb.gov/pressrel/2004/040226.htm (accessed 25 May 2005).

5. Baum Hedlund, "Companies Accept Responsibility and Publicly Apologize to the Families of the January 8, 2003 Air Midwest Flight 5481 Crash in Charlotte, North Carolina," 6 May 2005, online at www.baumhedlundlaw.com/media/aviation/air midwestapology.htm (accessed 25 May 2005).

6. BP Products North America, "BP Products North America Accepts Responsibility for Texas City Explosion," 17 May 2005, online at bpresponse.org (accessed 5 June 2005).

7. Anne Belli, "BP to Pay Millions to Families in Blast," *Houston Chronicle*, 23 June 2005, online at www.chron.com/cs/cda/ssistory.mpl/special/05/blast/3237407 (accessed 12 July 2005).

8. Anne Belli, "Safety Board Finds Failure of BP Alarms," *Houston Chronicle*, 29 June 2005, online at www.chron.com/cs/cda/ssistory.mpl/special/05/blast/3245476 (accessed 12 July 2005).

9. BP Products North America, 2.

10. Phillip Matier and Andrew Ross, "Training Video Prequel: 49ers Apologize Anew," *San Francisco Chronicle*, 8 June 2005, sec. A, p. 1.

11. Matier and Ross, 1.

12. Denise York and John York, "Statement from Denise and John York," 1 June 2005, online at www.sf49ers.com (accessed 5 June 2005).

13. De'Ann Weimer, "EEOC Sexual Harassment at Mitsubishi is 'Unprecedented,'" *Business Week Online*, 16 Sept. 1997, online at www.businessweek.com/bwdaily/dnflash/september/nf70916a.htm (accessed 12 July 2005).

14. Ceci Rodgers, "Mitsubishi Management Knocked," *CNN-Money*, 12 Feb. 1997, online at money.cnn.com/1997/02/12/busunu/mitsubishi_pkg (accessed 12 July 2005).

15. Weimer, para. 4.

16. Tyco, "Tyco Files Suit against Former Chairman and CEO L. Dennis Kozlowski for Misappropriating Money and Assets from the Company," 12 Sept. 2002, online at www.tyco.com (accessed 8 May 2005).

17. Tyco, "Tyco Releases Letter to Employees from Newly Appointed Chairman and CEO Edward D. Breen," 1 Aug. 2002, online at www.tyco.com (accessed 8 May 2005).

18. Tyco, "Letter," para. 8.

19. Carl Rotenberg, "Tyco Exec: Ethics Matter," *Times Herald.com*, 13 Nov. 2004, online at www.timesherald.com (accessed 8 May 2005).

CHAPTER 5

1. Fink, 20–22.

2. Edmund Sanders, Judy Paternak, and John O'Dell, "State Farm Says It Alerted Firestone to Problem," *Los Angeles Times*, 16 Aug. 2000, Home Edition, C-1.

3. Devon Spurgeon, "State Farm Researcher's Sleuthing Helped Prompt Firestone Recall," *Wall Street Journal*, 1 Sept. 2000, B-1.

4. Ian I. Mitroff, Christine M. Pearson, and L. Katherine Harrington, *The Essential Guide to Corporate Crises: A Step-by-Step Handbook for Surviving Major Catastrophes* (New York: Oxford University Press, 1996), 111–116.

5. Bert Case, "Nissan Uses Device to Stop Hail," WLBT TV (Jackson, MS), Feb. 2004, online at www.wlbt.com (accessed 20 July 2005).

6. George Tibbals, *The* Titanic: *The Extraordinary Story of the "Unsinkable" Ship* (Pleasantville, NY: Reader's Digest, 1997), 63–73.

7. Emily Gersema, "Experts Warn on Food Supply Attack," Police Policy Studies Council, 20 Sept. 2002, online at www.the ppsc.org/archives/terrorism/preparedness/experts_warn_on_food_ supply_threat.htm (accessed 21 Sept. 2002).

8. Vicky Gordon Martin and Donald R. Martin, "The Types and Styles of Managerial Information Scanning," *Management Communication Quarterly* 2 (1989): 392.

9. Joseph E. McCann II and Marilyn Buckner, "Strategic Integrating Knowledge Management Initiative," *Journal of Knowledge Management* 8 (2004): 45–50.

10. Dan Vergano, "Scientists in US Saw Tsunami Coming," *USA Today*, 28 Dec. 2004, 10-A.

11. "U.K. Girl Saved Tourists after Raising Warning," Yahoo! News, 2 Jan. 2005, online at uk.news.yahoo.com (accessed 5 Jan. 2005).

12. Goran Milenkovic, "Early Warning of Organizational Crises: A Research Project from the International Air Express Industry," *Journal of Communication Management*, 5 (2001): 362.

13. Coombs, 32–33.

14. Milenkovic, 364.

CHAPTER 6

1. Coombs, 68–69.

2. Coombs, 69.

3. Federal Emergency Management Agency (FEMA), *Exercise Design* (Washington, DC: U.S. Government Printing Office, 2003), 1.1.

4. FEMA, *Exercise*, 1.4.

5. FEMA, *Exercise*, 1.2.

6. FEMA, *Exercise*, 2.5–2.17.

7. FEMA, "Are You Ready," 2003, online at www.fema.gov/pdf/areyouready_full.pdf (accessed 29 Oct. 2003).

8. National Institute for Occupational Safety and Health, *Respirator Fact Sheet* (Atlanta, GA: National Institute for Occupational Safety and Health, 2003), 1–3.

9. Nicole Ross, "Terrorism: How Will It Impact Contingency Planning?" *Contingency Planning Management* 6.5 (2001): 14–17.

CHAPTER 7

1. Nick Morgan, "Do You Have Change Fatigue?" Harvard Business School Working Knowledge Home Page, 10 Sept. 2001, online at hbswk.hbs.edu (accessed 16 Jan. 2005).

2. Michael Tushman and Charles O'Reilly, "Leading Change and Organizational Renewal," Harvard Business School Working Knowledge Home Page, 16 Nov. 1999, online at hbswk.hbs.edu (accessed 16 Jan. 2005).

3. Vernon D. Miller, John R. Johnson, and Jennifer Grau, "Antecedents to Willingness to Participate in a Planned Organizational Change," *Journal of Applied Communication Research* 22 (1994): 59–60.

4. Tushman and O'Reilly, para. 6–7.

5. Art Kleiner, "The Few, the Proud, the In Crowd," Harvard Business School Working Knowledge Home Page, 4 Aug. 2003, online at hbswk.hbs.edu (accessed 16 Jan. 2005).

6. Morgan, para. 5.

7. Miller et al., p. 64.

8. Eric Abrahamson, "Change without Pain: Dynamic Stability," Harvard Business School Working Knowledge Home Page, 11 Sept. 2000, online at hbswk.hbs.edu (accessed 16 Jan. 2005).

9. Morgan, para. 5.

References

Abrahamson, Eric. "Change without Pain: Dynamic Stability." Harvard Business School Working Knowledge Home Page, 11 Sept. 2000. Online at hbswk.hbs.edu (accessed 16 Jan. 2005).

"Babe Star Arrested at Wendy's Protest." PETA, 3 July 2001. Online at www.peta.org/feat/wendys/warnshot.html (accessed 18 June 2005).

Barton, Laurence. *Crisis in Organizations II.* Cincinnati, OH: Thompson Learning, 2001.

Baum, Hedlund. "Companies Accept Responsibility and Publicly Apologize to the Families of the January 8, 2003 Air Midwest Flight 5481 Crash in Charlotte, North Carolina." 6 May 2005. Online at www.baumhedlundlaw.com/media/aviation/airmidwestapology.htm (accessed 25 May 2005).

Belli, Anne. "BP to Pay Millions to Families in Blast." *Houston Chronicle*, 23 June 2005. Online at www.chron.com (accessed 12 July 2005).

Belli, Anne. "Safety Board Finds Failure of BP Alarms." *Houston Chronicle*, 29 June 2005. Online at www.chron.com (accessed 12 July 2005).

"Bill Zavertnik." Chi-Chi's, 22 Nov. 2003. Online at www.chi-chis.com (accessed 1 Dec. 2003).

BP Products North America, Inc. "BP Products North America Accepts Responsibility for Texas City Explosion." 17 May 2005. Online at bpresponse.org (accessed 5 June 2005).

Bridis, Ted. "Study Examines Motives for Office Sabotage." *Miami Herald,* 17 May 2005. Online at www.miami.com (accessed 21 June 2005).

"Burger King Ads to Warn about Toys." Associated Press, 28 Jan. 2000. *Lexis-Nexis Academic* (accessed 17 May 2005).

"Burger King Recall of Pokemon Toy not Thorough Enough." Associated Press, 28 Dec. 1999. *Lexis-Nexis Academic* (accessed 17 May 2005).

Case, Bert. "Nissan Uses Device to Stop Hail." WLBT, Feb. 2004. Online at www.wlbt.com (accessed 20 July 2005).

Cebrzynski, Gregg. "Experts Say Pokemon Recall Unlikely to Tarnish Burger King's Image." *Nation's Restaurant News*, 34.2 (2000).

"Chi-Chi's, Inc. Comments on the Dismissal of Three Lawsuits." Chi-Chi's, 1 Dec. 2003. Online at www.chi-chis.com (accessed 12 Jan. 2004).

"ChoicePoint: More ID Theft Warning." *CNNMoney*, 17 Feb. 2005. Online at money.cnn.com (accessed 15 May 2005).

Coombs, W. Timothy. *Ongoing Crisis Communication: Planning, Managing, and Responding.* Thousand Oaks, CA: Sage, 1999.

Coombs, W. Timothy. "West Pharmaceutical's Explosion: Structuring Crisis Discourse Knowledge." *Public Relations Review* 30 (2004): 467–473.

Coombs, W. Timothy, and Sherry J. Holladay. "Helping Crisis Managers Protect Reputational Assets: Initial Tests of the Situational Crisis Communication Theory." *Management Communication Quarterly* 16 (2002): 176–181.

Coombs, W. Timothy, and Sherry J. Holladay. "Reasoned Action in Crisis Communication: An Attribution Theory-Based Approach to Crisis Management," in *Responding to Crisis: A Rhetorical Approach to Crisis Communication*, eds. Dan P. Millar and Robert L. Heath. Mahwah, NJ: Lawrence Elrbaum, 2004.

Cullen, Francis T., William Maakestad, and Gary Cavender. *Corporate Crime under Attack: The Ford Pinto Case and Beyond.* Cincinnati, OH: Anderson, 1987.

Dalesio, Emery P. "Investigators Look at Dust Build-up, Unknown Spark in Factory Blast." Associated Press, 4 Feb. 2003. Online at www.ap.org (accessed 8 Feb. 2003).

Devlin, Ed. "A Top Consultant Discusses the Bombing of the World Trade Center." *Disaster Recovery Journal* 6, no. 2 (1993). Online at www.drj.com/special/wtc/w2_036.htm (accessed 12 June 2005).

Dooley, Kerry, and Kristen Hallam. "Merck Stock Plummets on Vioxx Report." *National Post's Financial Post & FP Investing*, 2 (Nov. 2004): 8.

Dowling, Grahame. *Creating Corporate Reputations: Identity, Image, and Performance.* New York: Oxford University Press, 2001.

Enriquez, Susana, and Donna Horowitz. "Finger Has Lunch Crowd Rethinking Its Choices." *Los Angeles Times*, 26 March 2005, sec. B, p. 1.

Federal Emergency Management Agency (FEMA). "Are You Ready." 2003. Online at www.fema.com/pdf/areyouready_full.pdf (accessed 29 October 2003).

Federal Emergency Management Agency (FEMA). *Exercise Design.* Washington, DC: U.S. Government Printing Office, 2003.

Fink, Steven. Crisis Management: *Planning for the Inevitable.* New York: American Management Association, 1986.

Gersema, Emily. "Experts Warn on Food Supply Attack." Police Policy Studies Council, 20 Sept. 2002. Online at www .theppsc.org/archives/terrorism/preparedness/experts_warn_ on_food_supply_threat.htm (accessed 21 Sept. 2002).

Gramling, Alex. "Spread of Internet Lies Spooks Large Organizations." *New York Times*, 28 May 1997. Online at www.alex gramling.net/nytimes.htm (accessed 12 June 2005).

Grice, Corey. "How a Basic Attack Crippled Yahoo." News.com, 7 Feb. 2000. Online at news.com (accessed 15 May 2005).

Heath, Robert L. "Public Relations," in *Encyclopedia of Public Relations*, ed. Robert L. Heath. Thousand Oaks, CA: Sage Publications, 2005.

Hopper, D. Ian. "Technology: Hacking up, Disclosure down, FBI Survey." Webprowire, 7 April 2002. Online at www.webprowire .com/summaries/62059.html (accessed 14 May 2005).

"Insider Threat Study: Computer System Sabotage in Critical Infrastructure Sectors." CERT, May 2005. Online at www.cert.org (accessed 21 June 2005).

"Judge OKs Rules for Hepatitis Claims." *Charleston Daily Mail*, 13 Dec. 2003, sec. C, p. 5.

Kleiner, Art. "The Few, the Proud, the In Crowd." *Harvard Business School Working Knowledge Home Page*, 4 Aug. 2003. Online at hbswk.hbs.edu (accessed 16 Jan. 2005).

Lockheed Martin. "Lockheed Martin Statement Regarding Shooting Incident at Meridian, Mississippi Subassembly Plant." 8 July 2003. Online at www.lockheedmartin.com/news/articles/070 803_2.html (accessed 12 Sept. 2003).

Macdonald, Kathy. "A New Frontier in Crime...Identity Theft," in *The Future Is Convergence: 2005 West Proceedings*, ed. Contingency Planning Management. Flemington, NJ: Witter Publishing, 2005.

Martin, Vicky Gordon, and Donald R. Martin. "The Types and Styles of Managerial Information Scanning." *Management Communication Quarterly* 2 (1989): 392.

Matier, Phillip, and Andrew Ross. "Training Video Prequel: 49ers Apologize Anew." *San Francisco Chronicle*, 8 June 2005, sec. A, p. 1.

McCann, Joseph E. II, and Marilyn Buckner. "Strategic Integrating Knowledge Management Initiative." *Journal of Knowledge Management* 8 (2004): 45–50.

McCarthy, Anne N. "No Plan, No Site, No Business." *Disaster Recovery Journal* 6, no. 2 (1993). Online at www.drj.com/special/wtc/w2_033.htm (accessed 12 June 2005).

"McDonald's Board of Directors Elects Charlie Bell President and CEO; Andrew J. McKenna Elected Non-Executive Chairman." McDonald's Corporation, 19 May 2004. Online at www.mcdonalds.com (accessed 20 June 2005).

"McDonald's Chairman and CEO Jim Cantalupo Passes Away." McDonald's Corporation, 19 May 2004. Online at www.mcdonalds.com (accessed 20 June 2005).

"Memorial Service." West Pharmaceuticals, 20 Feb. 2003. Online at investor.westpharma.com (accessed 21 July 2003).

Messmer, Ellen. "The Anti-DDoS Prescription." *Network World*, 24 Sept. 2001. Online at www.networkworld.com/buzz2001/anti ddos (accessed 14 May 2005).

Milenkovic, Goran. "Early Warning of Organizational Crises: A Research Project from the International Air Express Industry." *Journal of Communication Management* 5 (2001): 362.

Miller, Vernon D., John R. Johnson, and Jennifer Grau. "Antecedents to Willingness to Participate in a Planned Organizational Change." *Journal of Applied Communication Research* 22 (1994): 59–60.

Mitroff, Ian I., Christine M. Pearson, and L. Katherine Harrington. *The Essential Guide to Corporate Crises: A Step-by-Step Handbook for Surviving Major Catastrophes* (New York: Oxford University Press, 1996).

Morgan, Nick. "Do You Have Change Fatigue?" *Harvard Business School Working Knowledge Home Page*, 10 Sept. 2001. Online at hbswk.hbs.edu (accessed 16 Jan. 2005).

National Institute for Occupational Safety and Health. "Respirator Fact Sheet." (Atlanta, GA: National Institute for Occupational Safety and Health, 2003), 1–3.

National Transportation Safety Board. "Loss of Pitch Control Caused Crash of Fatal Airliner Crash in Charlotte, North Carolina Last Year." NTSB, 26 Feb. 2004. Online at www.ntsb.gov/pressrel/2004/040226.htm (accessed 25 May 2005).

"NTSB Concludes TWA Flight 800 Probe." CBS, 4 August 2000. Online at www.cbsnews.com/stories/2000/03/24/world/main227488.shtml (accessed 20 July 2005).

"Patient Safety." *Heart Disease Weekly* (31 October 2004): 196.

"PETA Wins 'Wicked Wendy's' Campaign." PETA, 6 Sept. 2001. Online at www.peta.org (accessed 18 June 2005).

Potter, Denise. "Hackers Capture Info from George Mason U." *USA Today*, 11 Jan. 2005. Online at www.usatoday.com (accessed 14 May 2005).

Poulsen, Kevin. "Hacker Penetrates T-Mobile Systems." Security Focus, 11 Jan. 2005. Online at www.securityfocus.com/news/10271 (accessed 12 May 2005).

"Preliminary Findings Confirms Blast at West Pharamaceutical Services in Kinston, NC Was a Dust Explosion." U.S. Chemical Safety Board, 18 June 2003. Online at www.chemsafety.gov/news/2003/n20030602.htm (accessed 31 July 2003).

Ray, Sally J. *Strategic Communication in Crisis Management: Lessons from the Airline Industry.* Westport, CT: Quorum Books, 1999.

"Reports of Blindness in Men Using Viagra, Cialis." *MSNCB.com*, 27 May 2005. Online at www.msnbc.com (accessed 27 May 2005).

"Response to Article by Juni et al. Published in *The Lancet* on Nov. 5." Merck, 7 November, 2004. Online at www.merck.com/state ment_2004_1105/lancet.pdf (accessed 10 Nov. 2004).

Rodgers, Ceci. "Mitsubishi Management Knocked." *CNNMoney*, 12 Feb. 1997. Online at money.cnn.com/1997/02/12/busunu/ mitsubishi_pkg (accessed 12 July 2005).

Ross, Nicole. "Terrorism: How Will It Impact Contingency Planning?" *Contingency Planning Management* 6.5 (2001): 14–17.

Rotenberg, Carl. "Tyco Exec: Ethics Matter." *TimesHerald.com*, 13 Nov. 2004. Online at www.timesherald.com (accessed 8 May 2005).

"Safety Recall." NESCO/American Harvest, 6 Nov. 2003. Online at www.nesco.com/safety_recall (accessed 12 Nov. 2003).

Sanders, Edmund, Judy Paternak, and John O'Dell. "State Farm Says It Alerted Firestone to Problem." *Los Angeles Times*, 16 Aug. 2000. Home Edition, C-1.

"Security Breach Could Affect 500,00 People Nation-Wide." Continuity e-Guide, 23 Feb. 2005. Online at disaster-resource.com (accessed 15 May 2005).

"Southern Baptists Vote for Disney Boycott." CNN, 18 June 1997. Online at www.cnn.com/US/9706/18/baptists.disney (accessed 20 June 2005).

Spurgeon, Devon. "State Farm Researcher's Sleuthing Helped Prompt Firestone Recall." *Wall Street Journal*, 1 Sept. 2000, B-1.

"Temporary Relocation." West Pharmaceuticals, 21 Feb. 2003. Online at investor.westpharma.com (accessed 21 July 2003).

Tibbals, George. The Titanic: *The Extraordinary Story of the "Unsinkable" Ship.* Pleasantville, NY: Reader's Digest, 1997.

Tierney, Catherine. "Workplace Shootings." *St. Louis Post-Dispatch*, 3 July 2003, sec. A, p. 7.

Tushman, Michael, and Charles O'Reilly. "Leading Change and Organizational Renewal." *Harvard Business School Working Knowledge Home Page*, 16 Nov. 1999. Online at hbswk.hbs.edu (accessed 16 Jan. 2005).

Tyco. "Tyco Files Suit against Former Chairman and CEO L. Dennis Kozlowski for Misappropriating Money and Assets from the Company." Tyco, 12 Sept. 2002. Online at www.tyco.com (accessed 8 May 2005).

Tyco. "Tyco Releases Letter to Employees from Newly Appointed Chairman and CEO Edward D. Breen." Tyco, 1 Aug. 2002. Online at www.tyco.com (accessed 8 May 2005).

"U.K. Girl Saved Tourists after Raising Warning." Yahoo! News, 2 Jan. 2005. Online at uk.news.yahoo.com (accessed 5 Jan. 2005).

"Update." West Pharmaceuticals, 4 Feb. 2003. Online at investor .westpharma.com (accessed 21 July 2003).

Vergano, Dan. "Scientists in US Saw Tsunami Coming." *USA Today*, 28 Dec. 2004, 10-A.

Weimer, De'Ann. "EEOC Sexual Harassment at Mitsubishi Is 'Unprecedented.'" *Business Week Online*, 16 Sept. 1997. Online at www.businessweek.com/bwdaily/dnflash/september/nf70916a .htm (accessed 12 July 2005).

"Wendy's Doubles Chili Finger Reward to $100,000." Reuters, 5 April 2005. Online at news.yahoo.com (accessed 15, May, 2005).

Williams, Martyn. "Ebay, Amazon, Buy.com Hit by Attacks." IDG News Service, 9 Feb. 2000. Online at www.nwfushion.com/ news/2000/0209attack.html (accessed 15 May 2005).

Willis, Simon, Laura Swanson, Luxman Satchi, and Kevin Thompson. "Design Defects of the Ford Pinto Gas Tank." Online at www.fordpinto.com/blowup.htm (accessed 25 May 2005).

"Woman in Wendy's Finger Case Arrested." Associated Press, 22 April 2005. Online at www.forbes.com (accessed 12 May, 2005).

York, Denise, and John York. "Statement from Denise and John York." 1 June 2005. Online at www.sf49ers.com (accessed 5 June 2005).

Index

About the Author

W. TIMOTHY COOMBS is Associate Professor in the Communication Studies Department, Eastern Illinois University, where he teaches courses in crisis management, corporate communications, and public relations. Previously on the faculty of Wayne State University, Clemson University, and Illinois State University, he is the author or coauthor of two textbooks, *Ongoing Crisis Communication* and *Today's Public Relations*, and dozens of articles in such publications as *Public Relations Review*, *Management Communication Quarterly*, and the *Journal of Public Affairs*. He also consults on issues of crisis management, communication, and public relations for clients in the petrochemical, construction/engineering, and healthcare industries.